THE HUMANISTIC TRADITION

5

From
Romanticism
to Realism
in the Western
World

THE HUMANISTIC TRADITION

5 From Romanticism to Realism in the Western World

Gloria K. Fiero

University of Southwestern Louisiana

WCB Brown & Benchmark

Book Team

Developmental Editor *Deborah Daniel Reinbold*
Production Editor *Daniel Rapp*
Designer *Elise A. Burckhardt*
Art Editor *Miriam J. Hoffman*
Permissions Editor *Mavis M. Oeth*
Art Processor *Andréa Lopez-Meyer*
Visuals/Design Developmental Consultant *Marilyn A. Phelps*

Brown &
Benchmark
A Division of Wm. C. Brown Communications, Inc.

Vice President and General Manager *Thomas E. Doran*
Executive Managing Editor *Ed Bartell*
Executive Editor *Edgar J. Laube*
Director of Marketing *Kathy Law Laube*
National Sales Manager *Eric Ziegler*
Marketing Manager *Kathleen Nietzke*
Advertising Manager *Jodi Rymer*
Managing Editor, Production *Colleen A. Yonda*
Manager of Visuals and Design *Faye M. Schilling*

Design Manager *Jac Tilton*
Art Manager *Janice Roerig*
Production Editorial Manager *Ann Fuerste*
Publishing Services Manager *Karen J. Slaght*
Permissions/Records Manager *Connie Allendorf*

Wm. C. Brown Communications, Inc.

Chairman Emeritus *Wm. C. Brown*
Chairman and Chief Executive Officer *Mark C. Falb*
President and Chief Operating Officer *G. Franklin Lewis*
Corporate Vice President, Operations *Beverly Kolz*
Corporate Vice President, President of WCB Manufacturing *Roger Meyer*

Main Cover Photograph:
Ludwig van Beethoven. Courtesy of the Free Library of
Philadelphia.

Cover Insets (top to bottom):
Voltaire in Old Age, Jean Antoine Houdon, Chateau de Versailles.
The Bettmann Archive.
Mint Marilyn Monroe, Andy Warhol, ca. 1962. Oil and silk
screen enamel on canvas. From the collection of Jasper Johns.
© 1992, The Estate and Foundation of Andy Warhol/A. R. S., New
York.
The White Cloud, Head Chief of the Iowas, George Catlin,
ca. 1845. Oil on canvas, 27¾ × 22¾ in. National Gallery of Art,
Washington, D.C. Paul Mellon Collection.

Copyeditor *Laura Beaudoin*

Photo Research by Kathy Husemann

The credits section for this book begins on page 117 and is
considered an extension of the copyright page.

BRIEF CONTENTS

EXPANDED CONTENTS
(BOOK 5)

PREFACE

I t's the most curious thing I ever saw in all my life!" exclaimed Lewis Carroll's Alice in Wonderland, as she watched the Cheshire Cat slowly disappear, leaving only the outline of a broad smile. "I've often seen a cat without a grin, but a grin without a cat!" A student encountering an ancient Greek epic, an African mask, or a Mozart opera—lacking any context for understanding these works—might be equally baffled. It may be helpful, therefore, to begin by explaining how the individual products (the "grin") of the humanistic tradition relate to the larger and more elusive phenomenon (the "cat") of human culture.

In its broadest sense, the term *humanistic tradition* refers to humankind's cultural legacy—the sum total of the significant ideas and achievements handed down from generation to generation. This tradition is the product of responses to conditions that have confronted all people throughout history. From earliest times, human beings have tried to ensure their own survival by controlling nature. They have attempted to come to terms with the inevitable realities of disease and death. They have devised methods of living collectively and communally. And they have persisted in the desire to understand themselves and their place in the universe. In response to these everpresent and universal challenges—*survival, communality,* and *self-knowledge*—human beings have created the tools of science and technology, social and cultural institutions, religious and philosophical systems, and various forms of personal expression—all of which we call *culture.*

Obviously, even the most ambitious survey cannot assess all of the manifestations of human culture. This text, therefore, focuses on the creative legacy referred to collectively as *the humanities:* literature, philosophy, history (in its literary dimension), architecture, the visual arts (including photography and film), music, and dance. Selected examples from each of these disciplines—though often abridged—constitute our *primary sources.* As works original to their age, the primary sources provide firsthand evidence of human inventiveness and ingenuity. The primary sources in this text have been chosen on the basis of their authority, their beauty, and their enduring value. They are, simply stated, the masterpieces of their time, and in some cases, of all time. They are, as well, the landmark examples of a specific people and place. As such, they offer insight into the ideas and values of the society in which they were produced. In order to delineate the entire "cat," the text also provides some discussion of the relevant political, economic, and social circumstances out of which the primary sources emerged.

The Humanistic Tradition explores ideas and values that belong to all of humankind; hence the text offers a global rather than exclusively Western perspective. Our multicultural approach maintains that the humanistic tradition is not the exclusive achievement of any one geographic region, race, or class of human beings. Yet, in the main, the primary sources examined in these pages were created by individuals with special sensitivities and unique talents for interpreting the conditions and ideals of their age. The drawings of Leonardo da Vinci, for example, reveal a passionate determination to understand the operations and functions of nature. And while Leonardo was far above average in his abilities, his efforts may be taken as a reflection of a robust curiosity that characterized his time and place—the Age of the Renaissance in Italy.

The Humanistic Tradition is a survey, not an exhaustive analysis of our creative legacy. The critical reader will discover many gaps, the most unfortunate of which is the relative lack of attention afforded the arts and ideas of Asia and Africa by comparison with those of the West. On the other hand, some aspects of Western culture that traditionally receive extended examination in humanities surveys have been pared down to make room for the often neglected contributions of Islam, Africa, China, and India. This book is necessarily selective—it omits many major figures and treats others only briefly. Primary sources are arranged, for the most part, chronologically, but they are treated in thematic or topical contexts. The intent is to examine the informing ideas of the humanistic tradition rather than to compile a series of minihistories of the individual arts.

The Legacy of the Humanistic Tradition

To study the creative record is to engage in a dialogue with the past, one that brings us face to face with the values of our ancestors and, ultimately, with our own values. Indeed, exploring the humanistic tradition is (or should be) a source of personal revelation; like Alice in Wonderland, our experiences will be enriched according to the degree of curiosity and patience we bring to them. Just as a lasting friendship with a special person benefits from extended familiarity, so our appreciation of a painting, a play, or a symphony benefits from repeated contact and close attention. There are no shortcuts to the appreciation of the humanistic tradition, but there are some techniques that may be helpful. We may, for instance, approach each primary source from the triple perspective of its *text,* its *context,* and its *subtext.*

The Text: The *text* of any primary source refers to its *medium* (what it is made of), its *form* (the shape it assumes), and its *content* (the subject it describes). All literature, for example, whether intended to be spoken or read, depends on the medium of words—the American poet Robert Frost once defined literature as "performance in words." Literary form varies according to the manner in which the words are arranged: for instance, dramatic dialogue, prose, or poetry. The main purpose of prose is to convey information, to narrate and describe, while poetry, which is founded on freedom from conventional patterns of grammar, is usually concerned with expressing emotions. Philosophy (the search for truth through reasoned analysis) and history (the record of the past) make use of prose to analyze and communicate ideas and information. In literature, as in most kinds of expression, content and form are usually interrelated. The subject matter or the form of a literary work usually determines its *genre.* For instance, a long narrative poem recounting the adventures of a hero is an *epic,* while a formal, dignified speech in praise of a person or thing constitutes a *eulogy.*

The visual arts—painting, sculpture, architecture, and photography—make use of such media as wood, clay, colored pigments, marble, granite, steel, and (more recently) plastic, neon, and computers. The style of the work of art depends on how the artist uses the formal elements of color, line, texture, and space—elements that lack denotative meaning. The formal elements of art may work to describe and interpret the visible world, as in such genres as portraiture and landscape painting. They may generate fantastic and purely imaginative kinds of imagery, or, they may be nonrepresentational—that is, completely without recognizable content. In general, however, the visual arts are all spatial—they operate and are apprehended in space.

The medium of music is sound. Like literature, music is a durational form of expression; that is, it is apprehended over the period of time in which it occurs, rather than "grasped" all at once. The formal elements of music include melody, rhythm, and harmony—elements that, like those of the visual arts, lack symbolic content. But while paintings and sculptures may imitate or describe nature, musical compositions are generally nonrepresentational. For that reason, music is the most difficult of the arts to describe in words. Dance is also a temporal art form. Its medium is the human body in its expressive dimension. Like music, dance is performance-oriented, but like painting and sculpture, dance unfolds in space as well as unfolds time.

In analyzing the text of a work of literature, art, or music, we might ask how its formal elements contribute to its meaning and affective power. We might also try to identify the style of the art work and ask whether and how that style reflects the personal vision of the artist. We may discover, moreover, that the creative artifacts of a specific period share certain defining features or characteristics. Similarities (both general and specific) between, for instance, Greek temples and Greek tragedies, between Chinese poems and paintings, or between postmodern fiction and pop sculpture may lead us to examine the relationship between such works of art and the cultures in which they were produced.

The Context: We use the word *context* to describe a historical and cultural milieu. In what time and place did the artifact originate? How did it function within the society in which it was created? Was the purpose of the piece decorative, didactic, magical, propagandistic? Did it serve the religious or political needs of the community? Sometimes our answers to these questions are mere guesses. Nevertheless, understanding the function of an artifact often serves to clarify the nature of its form (and vice versa). For instance, because much of the literature produced prior to the fifteenth century was spoken or chanted rather than read, that literature tends to feature repetition and rhyme, devices that facilitated memorization. We may assume that literary works embellished with frequent repetitions, such as the *Epic of Gilgamesh,* were products of an oral tradition. Then too, establishing the function of an artwork permits us to determine whether the created object satisfied an individual impulse or a communal need: the paintings on the walls of Paleolithic caves, which are among the most compelling animal illustrations in the history of world art, probably belonged to a sacred hunting ritual, the performance of which was essential to the survival of the community. Understanding the relationship between text and context is one of the principal concerns of any inquiry into the humanistic tradition.

The Subtext: The *subtext* of the literary or artistic object refers to its secondary and implied meanings. The subtext reveals the emotional or intellectual messages embedded in a work of art. The epic poems of the ancient Greeks, for instance, celebrate the virtues of male prowess and physical courage. State portraits of the seventeenth-century King Louis XIV of France carry a message of absolute and unassailable power. And, more recently, Andy Warhol's serial adaptations of Campbell's soup cans and Coca-Cola bottles mock the supermarket mentality of American culture. Analyzing the subtext of a work of art often involves an understanding of the implicit and explicit symbolism common to a particular age.

Beyond *The Humanistic Tradition*

This text is able to offer only small, enticing samples from an enormous cultural buffet. Students are encouraged to go beyond the tidbits provided here—to dine more fully from the table. And to feast most sumptuously, nothing can substitute for firsthand experience. Students, therefore, should make every effort to visit art museums and galleries, concert halls, and libraries. *The Humanistic Tradition* is written for typical students, who may or may not be able to read music but who surely are able to cultivate an appreciation of music in performance. The clefs that appear in the text refer to music listening selections listed at the end of each chapter and found on the accompanying cassettes, available from Wm. C. Brown Communications, Inc. The terms that appear in bold print in the text are defined in glossaries following each chapter. A list of suggestions for further reading also appears at the end of each chapter, while a selected general bibliography appears at the end of each book.

Acknowledgments

Writing *The Humanistic Tradition* has been an exercise in humility. Without the assistance of learned friends and colleagues, assembling a book of this breadth would have been an impossible task. James H. Dormon read all parts of the manuscript and made extensive and substantive editorial suggestions; as his colleague, friend, and wife, I am most deeply indebted to him. I am grateful to the following faculty members of the University of Southwestern Louisiana for their thoughtful suggestions: for literature, Allen David Barry, Darrell Bourque, C. Harry Bruder, John W. Fiero, Emilio F. Garcia, Doris Meriwether, John Moore, and Patricia K. Rickels; for history, Vaughan B. Baker, Ora-Wes S. Cady, and Thomas D. Schoonover; for philosophy, Steven Giambrone and Robert T. Kirkpatrick; for architecture, Ethel Goodstein; for geography, Tim Reilly; for science, John R. Meriwether; and for music, James Burke and Robert F. Schmalz.

The following readers and reviewers generously shared their insights in matters of content and style: Michael K. Aakhus (University of Southern Indiana–Evansville); Vaughan B. Baker (University of Southwestern Louisiana); Katherine Charlton (Mt. San Antonio Community College); Bessie Chronaki (Central Piedmont Community College); Debora A. Drehen (Florida Community College–Jacksonville); Paula Drewek (Macomb Community College); William C. Gentry (Henderson State University); Kenneth Ganza (Colby College); Ellen Hofman (Highline Community College); Burton Raffel (University of Southwestern Louisiana); Frank La Rosa (San Diego City College); George Rogers (Stonehill College); Douglas P. Sjoquist (Lansing Community College); Howard V. Starks (Southeastern Oklahoma State University); Ann Wakefield (Academy of the Sacred Heart—Grand Coteau); Sylvia White (Florida Community College–Jacksonville); and Audrey Wilson (Florida State University).

The University of Southwestern Louisiana facilitated my lengthy commitment to this project with two Summer Faculty Research Grants, as well as with an enormous measure of moral support. I am indebted to the energetic staff of Dupré Library, to the University Honors Program, which made available to me the research assistance of Kara D. DeRamus, Beth Jones, and Judy Guillot, and to the secretarial staff of the Department of History and Philosophy, especially Harriet Laporte, for her untiring and cheerful assistance. In preparing the time lines for the text, I have depended upon Glenn Melancon and the USL History Graduate Program. Special thanks go to the efficient personnel and staff of Wm. C. Brown Communications, Inc., and, in particular, to Acquisitions Editor Meredith M. Morgan, whose good humor and judicious advice lightened my burdens; and to Production Editor Dan Rapp, for his perfectionism and his unflagging support. Finally, I am deeply grateful to my students; their sense of wonder and enthusiasm for learning are continuing reminders of why this book was written.

Supplements for the Instructor

In addition to the books, a number of useful supplements are available to instructors using *The Humanistic Tradition*. Please contact your WCB representative for more information about these resources.

Instructor's Resource Manual

The Instructor's Resource Manual, written by Candace Waltz of San Diego City College, is designed to assist instructors as they plan and prepare for their classes. Possible course organizations and sample syllabi for semester or quarter systems are suggested. Each chapter corresponds to a chapter in the books, and features a chapter summary, chapter outline, and study questions, all designed to allow instructors to remove and copy as handouts for their students. There are two types of study questions: *Factual Questions* that allow students to recapture the important points of each chapter, and *Challenge Questions* that force students to think more deeply and critically about the subject matter. Each chapter has a correlation list that directs instructors to the appropriate music examples, slides, transparencies, and software sections of the other supplements. A list of suggested videotapes, recordings, videodiscs and their suppliers is included. The final section of the Resource Manual contains a Test Item File, divided by chapter and featuring multiple choice, true/false, short answer, and essay questions.

WCB TestPak 3.0

WCB TestPak, a computerized testing service, provides instructors with either a mail-in/call-in testing program or the complete test item file on diskette for use with IBM PC, Apple, or Macintosh computers. WCB QuizPak, part of TestPak, provides students with true/false and multiple choice questions for each chapter. These questions will be the same questions found on the TestPak service, so students can prepare for examinations. WCB GradePak, also a part of TestPak, is a computerized grade management system for instructors. This program tracks student performance on examinations and assignments. It will compute each student's percentage and corresponding letter grade, as well as class average.

Audiocassettes

Two ninety-minute audiocassettes are available for *The Humanistic Tradition*. Cassette One corresponds to music listening selections discussed in Books 1–3 and Cassette Two for music in Books 4–6. Each selection on the cassettes is discussed in the text and includes a voice introduction for easier location. These cassettes can be packaged with any of the six texts, or sold separately.

WCB Slide Bank

Available through Sandak, Inc., this customized slide set allows each instructor to choose slides that directly correspond to the text, or additional slides to illustrate similar concepts. Prices for the sets depend upon the total number of slides ordered. Contact your WCB representative for order forms and details.

WCB Humanities Transparencies

A set of 71 acetate transparencies is available with *The Humanistic Tradition*. These show examples of art concepts, architectural styles, art media, maps, musical notation, musical styles, and musical elements.

Culture 1.0 ©

Developed by Cultural Resources, Inc., for courses in interdisciplinary humanities, Culture 1.0 © is a fascinating journey into humanity's cultural achievements on Hypercard © software. Available in either IBM PC or Macintosh formats, this seven-disk program allows students to explore the achievements of humanity through essays, almanacs, visual, or musical examples. Each time period contains historical, political, religious, philosophical, artistic, and musical categories, creating an interactive, Socratic method of learning for the students. Culture 1.0 © also features note-taking capabilities, report capabilities, and a student workbook for more guided learning. Contact your WCB representative for preview disks or ordering information.

	To 1790	1800	1810	1820	1830	1840
WORLD EVENTS	French Revolution	Napoleon (crowned emperor 1804)————— *Code Napoleon* *Diary*		Turko-Greek War	July Revolution, 1830	Britain in India, W. Indies, China, Africa, and
		Industrialism——— England builds first steam railway locomotive, 1804			First Opium War Britain vs. China	
			U.S.-British War of 1812		First railway in France	
		Fulton: steamboat Jefferson inaugurated President of the U.S.			Morse: telegraph experiments in photography	
LITERATURE AND PHILOSOPHY	Romanticism ——————————————————→					
	Rousseau: *Confessions*		Shelley: "Ode to the West Wind" Keats: "Ode on a Grecian Urn" Byron: "Don Juan"; "Prometheus"		Cooper: *Frontier Tales* Poe: mysteries	
		Wordsworth: "Tintern Abbey"				
		Coleridge: *Lyrical Ballads*	M. Shelley: *Frankenstein*		Sand: *Lélia* Brontë: *Wuthering Heights*	
		Goethe: *Faust*		Bentham: Utilitarianism		
			Historical Novels: Scott Dumas		Schopenhauer	
				Hegel: dialectic; *Philosophy of History*		
VISUAL ARTS AND ARCHITECTURE	Neoclassicism ———————————					
	Romanticism ——————————————————→					
	David: *Napoleon Crossing St. Bernard Pass*	Gros: *Napoleon Visiting the Pest House at Jaffa*	Géricault: *Raft of Medusa*	Constable: *Wivenhoe Park*	Delacroix: *Liberty Leading the People*	
			Goya: *Third of May, 1808; Disasters of War*	Turner: *Snowstorm* Friedrich: *Two Men Looking at the Moon*	Rude: *The Volunteers of 1792*	
					Hudson River School Cole: *Oxbow* Bierstadt: *Rocky Mountains*	
				Japanese woodblock prints	first cast iron suspension bridge	
MUSIC AND DANCE		Beethoven: *Eroica* (Third Symphony); sonatas; string quartets		invention of iron frame piano	Chopin: *Étude in G-Flat Major*	
		Schubert: *lieder; Gretchen am Spinnrade*			Taglioni: *prima ballerina* *Les Sylphides*	

1840	1850	1860	1870	1880	1890	1900

——— Queen Victoria of England ———————————————————————————

New Zealand

Great Exhibition of London 1851

American Civil War

Maxwell: *Electricity and Magnetism*

processed steel aluminum, steam turbine, pneumatic tire and machine gun

Paris World Exhibition of 1889

Sino-Japanese War

U.S. transcontintal railroad

Revolutions of 1848

Britain legalizes labor unions

U.S. warships enter Tokyo harbor

steel-framed skyscraper

Helmholtz: First Law of Thermodynamics

Franco-Prussian War

Edison: incandescent light bulb; motion picture camera

Chevreul: *Principles of Harmony and Contrast*

electric elevator invented

Bell: telephone

Ford: motorcar

——————— Realism ———————

Proudhon: Utopian Socialism

Marx and Engels: *Communist Manifesto*

Emerson: *On Nature*

Whitman: free verse; *Leaves of Grass*

Transcendentalism

Thoreau: *Walden*

Darwin: *Origin of Species*

Tolstoy: *War and Peace*

Twain: *Adventures of Huckleberry Finn*

Carlyle: *On Heroes and Hero Worship*

Melville: *Moby Dick*

Social Darwinism "scientism"

Ibsen: *A Doll's House*

Bergson: *Time and Freewill*

Heine: *You Are Just Like a Flower*

Flaubert: *Madame Bovary*

Dostoevsky: *Crime and Punishment*

Zola: *Nana*

Symbolist poetry

Dickens: *Oliver Twist; The Old Curiosity Shop; Nicholas Nickleby; David Copperfield*

Hugo: *Les Misérables*

Mallarmé: *"L'Après midi d'un faune"*

Mill: *On Liberty; Subjection of Women*

Barry and Pugin: Houses of Parliament

Catlin: *Head Chief*

Corot: landscapes

Carpeaux: *The Dance*

Garnier: Paris Opera House

Art Nouveau: Horta Tiffany

Eiffel Tower

——————— Realism ———————

Courbet: *Burial at Ornans*

Daumier: *Third Class Carriage*

Manet: *Déjeuner sur l'herbe; Olympia*

Harnett: *Card Rack*

Eakins: *Agnew Clinic*

Homer: *Country School*

Sullivan: Guaranty Building

Brady: Civil War photography

Millet: *The Gleaners*

——— Impressionism ———

Monet: *Impression: Sunrise*

——— Postimpressionism ———

Van Gogh: *Starry Night*

Gauguin: *Day of the God*

Paxton: Crystal Palace

Japanese prints Europe

Renoir: *Moulin de la Galette*

Cassatt: *The Bath*

Degas: *Little Dancer*

Rodin: *Gates of Hell*

Seurat: *La Grand Jatte*

Toulouse-Lautrec: *Moulin Rouge*

Cézanne: *Mont Ste. Victoire*

Berlioz: *Symphony fantastique;* program music; *Harold in Italy*

Helmholtz: *On the Sensation of Tone*

Liszt: *Faust Symphony*

verismo

Tchaikovsky: *Romeo and Juliet; Swan Lake*

Puccini: *La Bohème*

Bizet: *Carmen*

Verdi: *Aida*

Wagner: music drama; *Der Ring des Nibelungen*

Duncan: mondern dance

Debussy: *Prelude to Afternoon of a Faun*

THE HUMANISTIC TRADITION

5 From Romanticism to Realism in the Western World

Introduction

Two fundamental developments influenced the cultural vitality of the nineteenth century. The first was the transformation of the West from an agricultural to an industrially based society. The second was the extension of European dominion over much of the rest of the world. During the nineteenth century, the population of Europe doubled in size, and material culture changed more radically than it had in the previous one thousand years. The application of science to practical invention had already sparked the beginnings of the Industrial Revolution—the mass production of material goods by machines. The first phase of this revolution occurred in mid-eighteenth-century England, with the development of the steam engine and the machinery for spinning and weaving textiles. But the revolution gained momentum during the nineteenth century, as the production of coal, iron, and steel encouraged the further expansion of industry and commerce. Industrialization involved a shift from the production of goods in homes and workshops to manufacture in factories, mills, and mines. It demanded enormous investments of capital and the efforts of a large labor force; it stimulated growth in Europe's urban centers. Finally, industrialism provided the basis for the West's controlling influence over the rest of the world.

If industrialism was the first of the shaping forces in nineteenth-century Western culture, the second was nationalism. Nationalism—the exaltation of the state—involved the patriotic identification of individuals with a territory that embraced a common language and history. As people began to identify political sovereignty with a nation rather than with the person of the ruler, they sought greater freedom from the autocratic political and economic restraints of the old ruling orders. They also rejected the efforts of other nations to control their destiny. Such sentiments underlay the revolutionary outbursts that were chronic and continuous throughout the nineteenth century. European nationalism spurred the drive toward unification within the Germanies and among the Italian provinces and gave rise to a pervasive militarism in the individual states of the West. In the course of the century, England, France, Germany, Belgium, and the United States increased in political, economic, and military strength; and Germany and Italy finally reached the status of unified nation-states.

The nineteenth century is often called "the romantic era." *Romanticism* may be defined as a movement in the history of culture, as an aesthetic style, and as an attitude or spirit. As a movement, romanticism involved a revolt against convention and authority and a search for freedom in personal, political, and artistic life. The romantics reacted against the orderly and systematic world view of the Enlightenment, the rationalism of Enlightenment culture, and the impersonality of growing industrialism. Estranged from traditional religious beliefs, the romantics looked upon nature as the dwelling place of God. They worked to revive their nation's history and to liberate the oppressed peoples of the earth.

As an artistic style, romanticism was a reaction against the neoclassical quest for order and intellectual control. Romantics favored the free expression of the imagination and the liberation of the emotions. In preference to aesthetic objectivity and formalism, romantics chose subjectivity and the spontaneous outpouring of feeling. They cultivated a taste for the exotic, the ecstatic, and the fantastic. Finally, as an attitude, romanticism may be seen as an effort to glorify the individual self by way of intuition and a reliance upon the senses. Romantics did not reject the value of reason; rather, they regarded the emotions as equally important to human experience. Sentimentality, nostalgia, melancholy, and longing were all characteristic of the romantic cast of mind.

The romantics saw themselves as the heroes and visionaries of their time. They freed themselves from exclusive dependence on the patronage of church and state and tended to pursue fiercely individualistic paths to creativity—paths that often alienated them from society. The lives and works of the romantics were marked by deep subjectivity—one might even say by self-indulgence. If the perceptions and passions of the romantics were intense, their desire to devise a language adequate to that intensity of feeling often drove them to frustration, despair, and, in the case of an unusual number of them, to an early death—the painters Gros and Géricault, the composers Chopin and Schubert, and the poets Byron, Shelley, and Keats all died before the age of forty.

Although romanticism dominated much of the nineteenth century, by 1850 a *realist* point of view began to challenge the romantic style. As a style, *realism* called for an objective and unidealized record of everyday life. Realism emerged partly in response to the social and economic effects of industrialism and partly as an expression of discontent with the contemporary political and economic order. As a movement, realism reflected popular demands for greater access to material wealth. In an age that weighed the benefits against the costs of modern technology, realists exhibited a profound sense of social consciousness and a commitment to contemporary problems of class and gender. Unlike the romantics, who felt alienated from society and often sought to escape oppressive materialism, realists saw themselves as men and women "of their time."

In the last quarter of the century, France emerged as the center of Western artistic productivity. Paris became a melting pot for artists and writers, many of whom turned their backs on both romanticism and realism. On the threshold of the twentieth century, artists became preoccupied with art as a language of form and feeling rather than as a vehicle of ideal beauty or moral truth.

Chapter 27, "The Romantic View of Nature," explores the centrality of nature and the natural in nineteenth-century literature, philosophy, and science. It examines nature as a source of inspiration in the poetry of Wordsworth, Shelley, Keats, and Whitman and in the intellectual achievements of Thoreau, Hegel, and Darwin. Chapter 28 deals with the role of the hero in romantic literature. Byron's *Prometheus* and Goethe's *Faust* provide the focus for a consideration of the ways in which the hero symbolized the individual and nationalistic ideals of the romantic artist. Chapter 29, "Romantic Themes in Art and Music," surveys the characteristic features of romantic painting, sculpture, architecture, music, and dance. The landscapes of Constable and Turner, the heroic themes of Gros and Géricault, and the impassioned invocations to liberty in the works of Goya, Delacroix, and Rude are among the principal topics in this chapter. The music of Beethoven, Schubert, Berlioz, and Chopin and the flowering of ballet and opera illustrate the vitality of European romanticism.

Chapter 30 examines the varieties of realism in the West during the second half of the nineteenth century. It deals with the dominant ideologies of liberalism and socialism and traces the shift from romanticism to realism in the literary works of Dickens, Flaubert, Ibsen, and in the paintings of Courbet and Manet. The final chapter in this unit, "Art for Art's Sake," explores changes in the arts during the last quarter of the nineteenth century. The symbolists and the impressionists tried to capture in art the fleeting sensations of life, while the postimpressionists van Gogh, Gauguin, Seurat, and Cézanne tested the expressive potential of form and color. These bold experiments bring us to the threshold of the twentieth century.

27

THE ROMANTIC VIEW OF NATURE

One of the central features of nineteenth-century romanticism was its love affair with nature and the natural. The romantics generally reacted against the artificiality of Enlightenment culture and the dismal effects of growing industrialism. In rural nature, they found a practical refuge from urban blight, smoke-belching factories, and poverty-ridden slums. Aesthetically, they perceived in nature, with all its shifting moods and rhythms, a metaphor for the romantic imagination. They looked to nature as the source of solace, inspiration, and self-discovery. In a broader sense, the romantic view of nature was nothing short of religious. With Rousseau, the romantics held that humans were by nature good but were corrupted by society. "Natural man" was one who was close to nature and unspoiled by social institutions. To such Enlightenment figures as John Locke, Alexander Pope, or Thomas Jefferson, nature had meant universal order, but to nineteenth-century romantics, nature was the source of divine ecstacy and the medium of the mystical bond that united God with the human soul. Romantics perceived unspoiled nature as the wellspring of all truth; many even viewed God and the natural universe as one. Such pantheism—more typical of Asian than of Western religious philosophy—characterized the writings of many European and American romantics, but it is most clearly exemplified in the poetry of William Wordsworth.

Wordsworth and the Poetry of Nature

Born in the Lake District of England, William Wordsworth (d. 1850) was the leading nature poet of the nineteenth century. Wordsworth dated the beginning of his career as a poet from the time—at age fourteen—when he was struck by the image of tree boughs silhouetted against a bright evening sky. Thereafter, "the infinite variety of natural appearances" became the principal source of his inspiration and the primary subject of his poetry. Wordsworth's consciousness of nature was part of his larger belief that through the senses, the individual could commune with elemental and divine universal forces.

In 1798 Wordsworth and his British contemporary Samuel Taylor Coleridge (d. 1834) produced the *Lyrical Ballads,* the literary work that marked the birth of the romantic movement in England. When the *Lyrical Ballads* appeared in a second edition in 1800, Wordsworth added a preface that formally explained the aims of romantic poetry. In this manifesto, Wordsworth defined poetry as "the spontaneous overflow of powerful feelings," which takes its origin "from emotion recollected in tranquillity." According to Wordsworth, the object of the poet was "to choose incidents and situations from common life [and] to throw over

FIGURE 27.1 *Interior of Tintern Abbey,* J. M. W. Turner, 1794. © The Board of Trustees of the Victoria and Albert Museum.

them a certain coloring of the imagination . . . and above all, to make these incidents and situations interesting by tracing in them, truly though not ostentatiously, the primary laws of our nature." Wordsworth championed a poetic language that resembled "the real language of men in a state of vivid sensation." Although he did not always abide by his own precepts, his rejection of the artificial diction of neoclassical verse in favor of "the real language of men" anticipated a new, more natural voice in poetry—one informed by childhood memories and deeply felt experiences recollected in tranquility. Wordsworth's verse reflects the romantic poet's fondness for **lyric poetry,** which—like art song—describes deep personal feeling.

One of the most inspired poems in the *Lyrical Ballads* is "Lines Composed a Few Miles Above Tintern Abbey," the product of Wordsworth's visit to the ruins of a medieval monastery situated on the banks of the Wye River in Southwest England (figure 27.1). The 159-line poem constitutes a paean to nature. Wordsworth begins by describing the sensations evoked by the countryside itself; he then muses on the pleasures and the solace that these memories provide as they are called up in recollection. The heart of the poem, however, is a joyous celebration of nature's moral value: nature allows the poet to "see into the life of things" (line 49), infuses him with "the still, sad music of humanity" (line 91), and ultimately brings him into the presence of the divine spirit.

Nature, he exults, is the "anchor" of his purest thoughts, the "nurse" and "guardian" of his heart and soul (lines 109–10). In the final portion of the poem (lines 112–59), he shares with his "dearest Friend," his sister Dorothy, the joys of his mystical communion with nature and humankind. In "Tintern Abbey," Wordsworth established three of the key motifs of nineteenth-century romanticism: the beneficent value of nature, the idea of nature's sympathy with human-kind, and the view that one who is close to nature is close to God.

READING 95　From Wordsworth's "Lines Composed a Few Miles Above Tintern Abbey"

Five years have passed; five summers, with the length
Of five long winters! and again I hear
These waters, rolling from their mountain-springs
With a soft inland murmur. Once again
Do I behold these steep and lofty cliffs,
That on a wild secluded scene impress
Thoughts of more deep seclusion; and connect
The landscape with the quiet of the sky.
The day is come when I again repose
Here, under this dark sycamore, and view   10
These plots of cottage-ground, these orchard tufts,
Which at this season, with their unripe fruits,
Are clad in one green hue, and lose themselves
'Mid groves and copses. Once again I see
These hedge-rows, hardly hedge-rows, little lines
Of sportive wood run wild: these pastoral farms,
Green to the very door; and wreaths of smoke
Sent up, in silence, from among the trees!
With some uncertain notice, as might seem
Of vagrant dwellers in the houseless woods,   20
Or of some Hermit's cave, where by his fire
The hermit sits alone.
　　　　　　　　　These beauteous forms,
Through a long absence, have not been to me
As is a landscape to a blind man's eye;
But oft, in lonely rooms, and 'mid the din
Of towns and cities, I have owed to them
In hours of weariness, sensations sweet,
Felt in the blood, and felt along the heart;
And passing even into my purer mind,   30
With tranquil restoration:—feelings too
Of unremembered pleasure: such, perhaps,
As have no slight or trivial influence
On that best portion of a good man's life,
His little, nameless, unremembered acts
Of kindness and of love. Nor less, I trust,
To them I may have owed another gift,
Of aspect more sublime; that blessed mood,
In which the burthen[1] of the mystery,

In which the heavy and the weary weight   40
Of all this unintelligible world,
Is lightened—that serene and blessed mood,
In which the affections gently lead us on—
Until, the breath of this corporeal frame
And even the motion of our human blood
Almost suspended, we are laid asleep
In body, and become a living soul;
While with an eye made quiet by the power
Of harmony, and the deep power of joy,
We see into the life of things.   50
　　　　　　　　　If this
Be but a vain belief, yet, oh! how oft—
In darkness and amid the many shapes
Of joyless daylight; when the fretful stir
Unprofitable, and the fever of the world,
Have hung upon the beatings of my heart—
How oft, in spirit, have I turned to thee,
O sylvan[2] Wye! thou wanderer through the woods,
How often has my spirit turned to thee!

　　And now, with gleams of half-extinguished thought,   60
With many recognitions dim and faint,
And somewhat of a sad perplexity,
The picture of the mind revives again;
While here I stand, not only with the sense
Of present pleasure, but with pleasing thoughts
That in this moment there is life and food
For future years. And so I dare to hope,
Though changed, no doubt, from what I was when first
I came among these hills; when like a roe
I bounded o'er the mountains, by the sides   70
Of the deep rivers, and the lonely streams,
Wherever nature led: more like a man
Flying from something that he dreads than one
Who sought the thing he loved. For nature then
(The coarser pleasures of my boyish days,
And their glad animal movements all gone by)
To me was all in all—I cannot paint
What then I was. The sounding cataract[3]
Haunted me like a passion; the tall rock,
The mountain, and the deep and gloomy wood,   80
Their colors and their forms, were then to me
An appetite; a feeling and a love,
That had no need of a remoter charm,
By thought supplied, nor any interest
Unborrowed from the eye. That time is past,
And all its aching joys are now no more,
And all its dizzy raptures. Not for this
Faint I, nor mourn nor murmur; other gifts
Have followed; for such loss, I would believe,
Abundant recompense. For I have learned   90
To look on nature, not as in the hour
Of thoughtless youth; but hearing oftentimes
The still, sad music of humanity,
Nor harsh nor grating, though of ample power
To chasten and subdue. And I have felt

[1]Burden.

[2]Wooded.
[3]A descent of water over a steep surface.

A presence that disturbs me with the joy
Of elevated thoughts; a sense sublime
Of something far more deeply interfused,
Whose dwelling is the light of setting suns,   100
And the round ocean and the living air,
And the blue sky, and in the mind of man:
A motion and a spirit, that impels
All thinking things, all objects of all thought,
And rolls through all things. Therefore am I still
A lover of the meadows and the woods,
And mountains; and of all that we behold
From this green earth; of all the mighty world
Of eye, and ear—both what they half create,
And what perceive; well pleased to recognize   110
In nature and the language of the sense,
The anchor of my purest thoughts, the nurse,
The guide, the guardian of my heart, and soul
Of all my moral being.
                            Nor perchance,
If I were not thus taught, should I the more
Suffer my genial spirits to decay:
For thou art with me here upon the banks
Of this fair river; thou my dearest Friend,[4]
My dear, dear Friend; and in thy voice I catch
The language of my former heart, and read   120
My former pleasures in the shooting lights
Of thy wild eyes. Oh! yet a little while
May I behold in thee what I was once,
My dear, dear Sister! and this prayer I make,
Knowing that Nature never did betray
The heart that loved her; 'tis her privilege,
Through all the years of this our life, to lead
From joy to joy: for she can so inform
The mind that is within us, so impress
With quietness and beauty, and so feed   130
With lofty thoughts, that neither evil tongues,
Rash judgments, nor the sneers of selfish men,
Nor greetings where no kindness is, nor all
The dreary intercourse of daily life,
Shall e'er prevail against us, or disturb
Our cheerful faith, that all which we behold
Is full of blessings.

                    . . . .

---

[4]Wordsworth's sister, Dorothy.

◆

Wordsworth introduced into English literature nature poetry—an idiom made famous by the Chinese (see chapter 14). Like the poets of the T'ang and Sung dynasties, Wordsworth found in nature a source of solitary joy and inspiration. For him, as for Li Po or Tu Fu, nature provided the tranquility essential to a state of contemplation. Chinese poets translated nature's moods by way of only a few carefully chosen words, evoking the subtlest of analogies between the external landscape and the human condition. Wordsworth, on the other hand, explored the moral implications of nature and its psychological effects upon the human spirit. Whereas the Chinese poet was content to describe the sensuous immediacy of nature, Wordsworth felt bound to distill the experience of the senses by way of the intellect, to discover moral analogues, and to put his personal feelings at the service of human instruction and improvement.

The Poetry of Shelley

Like Wordsworth, the British poet Percy Bysshe Shelley (d. 1822) regarded nature as the source of sublime truth. Shelley was a prolific writer and an outspoken champion of human liberty. His writings were intensely personal and his life had all the features of the romantic hero (see chapter 28). Defiant and unconventional, Shelley wrote the treatise *The Necessity of Atheism,* which led to his expulsion from Oxford University. He was outspoken in his opposition to marriage, which he viewed as hostile to human happiness. And, while married to one woman (Harriet Westbrook), he ran off with another (Mary Godwin). A critic of England's rulers, he went into permanent exile in Italy in 1818 and died there four years later in a boating accident.

Shelley's *Defense of Poetry,* a manifesto of the poet's function in society, hailed poets as "the unacknowledged legislators of the world." According to Shelley, poets took their authority from nature, the fountainhead of inspiration.

Shelley found in nature's moods metaphors for insubstantial, yet potent, human states. In "Ode to the West Wind," he appeals to the wind, a symbol of creativity, to drive his visions throughout the universe, as the wind drives leaves over the earth (stanza 1), clouds through the air (stanza 2), and waves on the seas (stanza 3). In the final stanza, Shelley compares the poet to a lyre, whose "mighty harmonies," stirred by the wind of creativity, will awaken the world. By means of language that is itself musical, Shelley defended the notion of poetry as the music of the soul. Consider, for instance, his frequent use of the exclamatory "O" and the tone color in lines 38 to 40: "while far below/The sea-blooms and the oozy woods which wear/The sapless foliage of the ocean, know."

READING 96 Shelley's "Ode to the West Wind"

1

O wild West Wind, thou breath of Autumn's being,
Thou, from whose unseen presence the leaves dead
Are driven, like ghosts from an enchanter fleeing,

Yellow, and black, and pale, and hectic red,
Pestilence-stricken multitudes: O thou,   5
Who chariotest to their dark wintry bed

The wingéd seeds, where they lie cold and low,
Each like a corpse within its grave, until
Thine azure sister of the spring shall blow

Her clarion o'er the dreaming earth, and fill   10
(Driving sweet buds like flocks to feed in air)
With living hues and odours plain and hill:

Wild Spirit, which art moving everywhere;
Destroyer and preserver; hear, oh, hear!

2

Thou on whose stream, 'mid the steep sky's commotion,   15
Loose clouds like earth's decaying leaves are shed,
Shook from the tangled boughs of Heaven and Ocean,

Angels of rain and lightning: there are spread
On the blue surface of thine aëry surge,
Like the bright hair uplifted from the head   20

Of some fierce Maenad,[5] even from the dim verge
Of the horizon to the zenith's height,
The locks of the approaching storm. Thou dirge

Of the dying year, to which this closing night
Will be the dome of a vast sepulchre,[6]   25
Vaulted with all thy congregated might

Of vapors, from whose solid atmosphere
Black rain, and fire, and hail will burst: O, hear!

3

Thou who didst waken from his summer dreams
The blue Mediterranean, where he lay,   30
Lulled by the coil of his crystalline streams,

Beside a pumice isle in Baiae's bay,[7]
And saw in sleep old palaces and towers
Quivering within the wave's intenser day,

All overgrown with azure moss and flowers   35
So sweet, the sense faints picturing them! Thou
For whose path the Atlantic's level powers

Cleave themselves into chasms, while far below
The sea-blooms and the oozy woods which wear
The sapless foliage of the ocean, know   40

Thy voice, and suddenly grow grey with fear,
And tremble and despoil themselves: O, hear!

4

If I were a dead leaf thou mightest bear;
If I were a swift cloud to fly with thee;
A wave to pant beneath thy power, and share   45

The impulse of thy strength, only less free
Than thou, O uncontrollable! If even
I were as in my boyhood, and could be

The comrade of thy wanderings over heaven,
As then, when to outstrip thy skiey speed   50
Scarce seemed a vision; I would ne'er have striven

As thus with thee in prayer in my sore need.
Oh! lift me as a wave, a leaf, a cloud!
I fall upon the thorns of life! I bleed!

A heavy weight of hours has chained and bowed   55
One too like thee: tameless, and swift, and proud.

5

Make me thy lyre, even as the forest is:
What if my leaves are falling like its own!
The tumult of thy mighty harmonies

Will take from both a deep, autumnal tone,   60
Sweet though in sadness. Be thou, spirit fierce,
My spirit! Be thou me, impetuous one!

Drive my dead thoughts over the universe
Like withered leaves to quicken a new birth!
And, by the incantation of this verse,   65

Scatter, as from an unextinguished hearth
Ashes and sparks, my words among mankind!
Be through my lips to unawakened earth

The trumpet of a prophecy! O, Wind,
If Winter comes, can Spring be far behind?   70

---

[5]A female attendant of Dionysus; a bacchante (see figure 26.12).
[6]Tomb.
[7]An ancient resort in Southwest Italy.

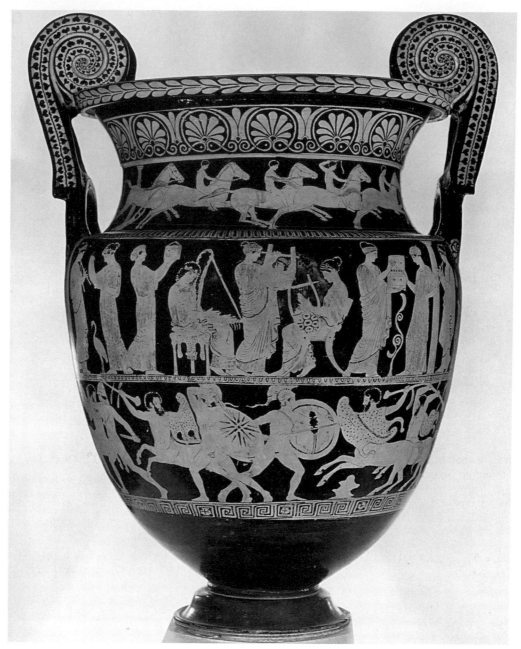

FIGURE 27.2 South Italian volute krater with women making music and centaur fight, Sisyphus painter, late fifth century B.C. Staatliche Antikensammlungen und Glyptothek, Munich.

The Poetry of Keats

The poetry of John Keats (d. 1821), the third of the three great British nature poets, shares the elegaic mood of romantic landscape painting. Keats lamented the transience of life's pleasures, even as he anticipated the brevity of life. He lost both his mother and his brother to tuberculosis, and he himself succumbed to that disease at the age of twenty-five. The threat of imminent death seems to have produced in Keats a heightened awareness of the virtues of beauty, human love, and friendship. Keats perceived these phenomena as fleeting forms of a higher reality made

permanent in art. For Keats, art was the great balm of the poet. Art was more than a response to the human experience of love and nature; it was the transmuted product of the imagination, a higher form of nature itself. These ideas are expressed in Keats' "Ode on a Grecian Urn." The poem was inspired by ancient Greek artifacts Keats had seen among those brought to London by Lord Elgin in 1816 and placed on display in the British Museum (figures 6.23, 6.24, and 6.25).

In the "Ode," Keats contemplates a Greek vase (much like the one pictured in figure 27.2), whose figures immortalize life's fleeting pleasures. The boughs of trees pictured on such a vase will never shed their leaves, the fair youths will never grow old, the music of the pipes and timbrels will never cease to play, and the lovers will never cease to love. The "little town by river" and the other pastoral vignettes in the poem probably did not belong to any one existing Greek vase; yet Keats describes the imaginary urn (his "Cold Pastoral") as a symbol of all great works of art, which, because of their unchanging beauty, remain eternally "true." The poem concludes with the joyous pronouncement that beauty and truth are one.

READING 97 Keats' "Ode on a Grecian Urn"

1

Thou still unravished bride of quietness,
  Thou foster-child of Silence and slow Time,
Sylvan historian, who canst thus express
  A flowery tale more sweetly than our rhyme:
What leaf-fringed[8] legend haunts about thy shape   5
  Of deities or mortals, or of both,
    In Tempe[9] or the dales of Arcady?[10]
  What men or gods are these? What maidens loth?
What mad pursuit? What struggle to escape?
    What pipes and timbrels? What wild ecstasy?   10

2

Heard melodies are sweet, but those unheard
  Are sweeter; therefore, ye soft pipes, play on;
Not to the sensual ear, but, more endeared,
  Pipe to the spirit ditties of no tone:
Fair youth, beneath the trees, thou canst not leave   15
  Thy song, nor ever can those trees be bare;
    Bold Lover, never, never canst thou kiss,
Though winning near the goal—yet, do not grieve;
    She cannot fade, though thou hast not thy bliss,
  For ever wilt thou love, and she be fair!   20

3

Ah, happy, happy boughs! that cannot shed
  Your leaves, nor ever bid the Spring adieu;
And, happy melodist, unwearièd,
  For ever piping songs for ever new;
More happy love! more happy, happy love!   25
  For ever warm and still to be enjoyed,
    For ever panting, and for ever young;
All breathing human passion far above,
  That leaves a heart high-sorrowful and cloyed,
    A burning forehead, and a parching tongue.   30

[8]A reference to the common Greek practice of bordering the vase with stylized leaf forms (see figure 27.2).
[9]A valley sacred to Apollo between Mounts Olympus and Ossa in Thessaly, Greece.
[10]Arcadia, the pastoral regions of ancient Greece (see Poussin's *Arcadian Shepherds*, figure 23.14).

4

Who are these coming to the sacrifice?
  To what green altar, O mysterious priest,
Lead'st thou that heifer lowing at the skies,
  And all her silken flanks with garlands drest?
What little town by river or sea shore,   35
  Or mountain-built with peaceful citadel,
    Is emptied of this folk, this pious morn?
And, little town, thy streets for evermore
  Will silent be; and not a soul to tell
    Why thou art desolate, can e'er return.   40

5

O Attic[11] shape! Fair attitude! with brede[12]
  Of marble men and maidens overwrought,
With forest branches and the trodden weed;
  Thou, silent form, dost tease us out of thought
As doth eternity: Cold Pastoral!   45
  When old age shall this generation waste,
    Thou shalt remain, in midst of other woe
Than ours, a friend to man, to whom thou say'st,
  "Beauty is truth, truth beauty,"—that is all
    Ye know on earth, and all ye need to know.   50

[11]Attica, a region in Southeastern Greece dominated by Athens.
[12]Embroidered.

American Romanticism: Transcendentalism

Across the Atlantic, along the eastern shores of the rapidly industrializing American continent, romanticism took hold both as an attitude of mind and as a style. Romanticism infused all aspects of nineteenth-century American culture: it distinguished the frontier tales of James Fenimore Cooper (d. 1851), the mysteries of Edgar Allan Poe (d. 1849), and the novels of Nathaniel Hawthorne (d. 1864) and Herman Melville (d. 1891). But it found its purest expression in a movement known as *transcendentalism*. The transcendentalists were a group of New England intellectuals who held that knowledge gained by way of intuition transcended or surpassed knowledge based on reason and logic. They believed that the direct experience of nature united one with God. They exalted individualism and self-reliance and urged that human beings discover their higher spiritual selves through sympathy with nature. Reacting against the material excesses of advancing industrialism, the transcendentalists embraced such antimaterialistic philosophies as neoplatonism (chapter 16), Asian mysticism (chapters 2 and 14), and German idealism (chapter

25). Though the transcendentalists were the descendants of English Puritans, they sought spiritual instruction in Eastern religious philosophies that had reached the Boston area in the early nineteenth century. From Hinduism and Buddhism, the transcendentalists adopted the idea that all people derived their being from the same universal source and therefore shared a "universal brotherhood"—the unity of humanity, nature, and God.

The prime exemplar of the transcendentalists was Ralph Waldo Emerson (d. 1882), whose familiar essays powerfully influenced nineteenth-century American thought. Like Wordsworth, Emerson courted nature to "see into the life of things" and to taste nature's cleansing power. In the essay entitled *Nature,* Emerson sets forth his pantheistic credo:

> In the woods is perpetual youth. Within these plantations of God, a decorum and sanctity reign, a perennial festival is dressed, and the guest sees not how he should tire of them in a thousand years. In the woods, we return to reason and faith. There I feel that nothing can befall me in life—no disgrace, no calamity (leaving my eyes), which nature cannot repair. Standing on the bare ground—my head bathed by the blithe air and uplifted into infinite space—all mean egotism vanishes. I become a transparent eyeball; I am nothing; I see all; the currents of the Universal Being circulate through me; I am part or parcel of God.[13]

Emerson's friend Henry David Thoreau (d. 1862) carried transcendentalism to its logical end by literally returning to nature. Thoreau had completed a degree at Harvard University and made his way in the world by tutoring, surveying, and making pencils. An avid opponent of slavery, he was jailed briefly for refusing to pay a poll tax to a proslavery government. In an influential essay on civil disobedience, he described the philosophy of passive resistance that he himself practiced—a philosophy embraced by the twentieth-century leaders Mohandas Karamchand Gandhi and Martin Luther King. In 1845 Thoreau abandoned urban society to live in the Massachusetts woods near Walden Pond—an experiment that lasted twenty-six months. He described his nonconformist attitude toward society and his deep commitment to monkish simplicity in his "handbook for living," called simply *Walden.* In this intimate yet forthright diary, from which the following excerpts are drawn, Thoreau glorifies nature as innocent and beneficent—a source of joy and practical instruction.

[13] *The Complete Essays and Other Writings of Ralph Waldo Emerson,* ed. Brooks Atkinson (New York: The Modern Library, 1950), 6.

READING 98   From Thoreau's *Walden*

Near the end of March, 1845, I borrowed an axe and went down to the woods by Walden Pond, nearest to where I intended to build my house, and began to cut down some tall, arrowy white pines, still in their youth, for timber. . . . It was a pleasant hillside where I worked, covered with pine woods, through which I looked out on the pond, and a small open field in the woods where pines and hickories were springing up. The ice in the pond was not yet dissolved, though there were some open spaces, and it was all dark-colored and saturated with water. There were some slight flurries of snow during the days that I worked there; but for the most part when I came out on to the railroad, on my way home, its yellow sand-heap stretched away gleaming in the hazy atmosphere, and the rails shone in the spring sun, and I heard the lark and pewee and other birds already come to commence another year with us. They were pleasant spring days, in which the winter of man's discontent was thawing as well as the earth, and the life that had lain torpid began to stretch itself. One day, when my axe had come off and I had cut a green hickory for a wedge, driving it with a stone, and had placed the whole to soak in a pond-hole in order to swell the wood, I saw a striped snake run into the water, and he lay on the bottom, apparently without inconvenience, as long as I stayed there, or more than a quarter of an hour; perhaps because he had not yet fairly come out of the torpid state. It appeared to me that for a like reason men remain in their present low and primitive condition; but if they should feel the influence of the spring of springs arousing them, they would of necessity rise to a higher and more ethereal life. I had previously seen the snakes in frosty mornings in my path with portions of their bodies still numb and inflexible, waiting for the sun to thaw them. On the 1st of April it rained and melted the ice, and in the early part of the day, which was very foggy, I heart a stray goose groping about over the pond and cackling as if lost, or like the spirit of the fog. . . .

I went to the woods because I wished to live deliberately, to front only the essential facts of life, and see if I could not learn what it had to teach, and not, when I came to die, discover that I had not lived. I did not wish to live what was not life, living is so dear; nor did I wish to practice resignation, unless it was quite necessary. I wanted to live deep and suck out all the marrow of life, to live so sturdily and Spartan-like as to put to rout all that was not life, to cut a broad swath and shave close, to drive life into a corner, and reduce it to its lowest terms, and, if it proved to be mean, why then to get the whole and genuine meanness of it, and publish its meanness to the world; or if it were sublime, to know it by experience, and be able to give a true account of it in my next excursion. For most men, it appears to me, are in a strange uncertainty about it, whether it is of the devil or of God, and have *somewhat hastily* concluded that it is the chief end of man here to "glorify God and enjoy him forever." . . .

• Simplicity, simplicity, simplicity! I say, let your affairs be as two or three, and not a hundred or a thousand; instead of a million count half a dozen, and keep your accounts on your thumb-nail . . . Instead of three meals a day, if it be necessary eat but one; instead of a hundred dishes, five; and reduce other things in proportion. • . . .

    The indescribable innocence and beneficence of Nature,—of sun and wind and rain, of summer and winter,—such health, such cheer, they afford forever! and such sympathy have they ever with our race, that all Nature would be affected, and the sun's brightness fade, and the winds would sigh humanely, and the clouds rain tears, and the woods shed their leaves and put on mourning in midsummer, if any man should ever for a just cause grieve. Shall I not have intelligence with the earth? Am I not partly leaves and vegetable mould myself? . . .

---◆---

Walt Whitman's Romantic Individualism

Though technically not a transcendentalist, Walt Whitman (d. 1892) gave voice to the transcendental worldview in his euphoric poetry (figure 27.3). Whitman followed Emerson's advice and lived according to the motto of self-reliance. He served as a male nurse in an American Civil War hospital and wrote articles and poems that celebrated his love for the American landscape. Like Wordsworth, Whitman took everyday life as his theme, but he rejected artificial poetic diction more completely than Wordsworth did. His natural voice bellowed a "barbaric yawp" that found ideal expression in **free verse** (poetry based on irregular rhythmic patterns rather than on the conventional use of meter). Whitman molded his bold rhythms and sonorous cadences by means of standard poetic devices, such as alliteration, assonance, and repetition. The musical grandeur of his verse simulated Italian opera, which Whitman loved; while his sprawling, cosmic images resembled nineteenth-century American landscapes (chapter 29). In "Song of Myself," the longest of the lyric poems included in the autobiographical collection called *Leaves of Grass,* we come face to face with the expansive individualism that typified the romantic movement. At the same time, we are struck by Whitman's impassioned quest for unity with nature and with all humanity.

FIGURE 27.3 *Walt Whitman,* Thomas Eakins, 1887–88. Oil on canvas, 30 in. × 24 in. Pennsylvania Academy of the Fine Arts, Philadelphia. General Fund 1917.1

READING 99   From Whitman's "Song of Myself"

1

I celebrate myself, and sing myself,
And what I assume you shall assume,
For every atom belonging to me as good belongs to
    you.

I loaf and invite my soul,
I learn and loaf at my ease observing a spear of summer   5
    grass.

My tongue, every atom of my blood, form'd from this
    soil, this air,
Born of parents born here from parents the same, and
    their parents the same,
I, now thirty-seven years old in perfect health begin,
Hoping to cease not till death.

Creeds and schools in abeyance,   10
Retiring back a while sufficed at what they are, but
    never forgotten,
I harbor for good or bad, I permit to speak at every
    hazard,
Nature without check with original energy.

The spotted hawk swoops by and accuses me, he
complains of my gab and my loitering.

I too am not a bit tamed, I too am untranslatable,
I sound my barbaric yawp over the roofs of the world.

The last scud of day holds back for me,
It flings my likeness after the rest and true as any on the   5
    shadow'd wilds,
It coaxes me to the vapor and the dusk.

I depart as air, I shake my white locks at the runaway
    sun,
I effuse my flesh in eddies, and drift it in lacy jags.

I bequeath myself to the dirt to grow from the grass I
    love,
If you want me again look for me under your boot-soles.   10

You will hardly know who I am or what I mean,
But I shall be good health to you nevertheless,
And filter and fibre your blood.

Failing to fetch me at first keep encouraged,
Missing me one place search another,   15
I stop somewhere waiting for you.

Romantic Philosophy: The Hegelian Dialectic

Romanticism found its formal philosophers largely among nineteenth-century German intellectuals. Johann Gottlieb Fichte (d. 1814), Georg Wilhelm Friedrich Hegel (d. 1831), and Arthur Schopenhauer (d. 1860) followed the philosophic idealism of Immanuel Kant (chapter 25) by exalting the role of the human mind in constructing an idea of the world. According to these thinkers, the truths of empirical experience were not self-evident, as Locke had argued, and the truths of the mind were not clear and distinct, as Descartes had held. The German idealists shared Rousseau's belief in the power of human instinct. And, much like Rousseau and the romantic poets, they viewed nature in deeply subjective terms. In Schopenhauer's pessimistic view, the only escape from a malignant reality was selfless contemplation, a concept inspired by his reading of Hindu philosophy and the mystical treatises of Meister Eckhart (chapter 15).

Welcoming the influence of Indian religious philosophy on European intellectuals, Schopenhauer wrote, "Sanskrit literature will be no less influential for our time than Greek literature was in the fifteenth century for the Renaissance." As self-scrutiny and a subjective analysis of the human mind came to provide the bases for philosophic theory, science and philosophy—allied in previous centuries—began to part company.

The most influential philosopher of the nineteenth century was Georg W. F. Hegel. A professor of philosophy at the University of Berlin, Hegel taught that the world consisted of a single divine nature, which he termed "absolute mind" or "spirit." According to Hegel, spirit and matter were involved in an evolutionary process impelled by spirit seeking to know its own nature. Hegel explained the operation of that process, or **dialectic**, as follows: every condition (or "thesis") confronts its opposite condition (or "antithesis"), which then generates a synthesis. The synthesis in turn produces its opposite, and so on, in a continuing evolution that moves, explained Hegel, toward the ultimate goal of spiritual freedom. For Hegel, all reality was a process that operated on the principle of the dialectic: thesis, antithesis, and synthesis, a principle that governed the realm of ideas, artistic creation, philosophical understanding, indeed, history itself. "Change in nature, no matter how infinitely varied it is," wrote Hegel, "shows only a cycle of constant repetition. In nature, nothing new happens under the sun."

In the dense prose work entitled *The Philosophy of History,* actually a compilation of his own and his students' lecture notes, Hegel advanced the idea that the essence of spirit is freedom, which finds its ultimate expression in the state. According to Hegel, human beings possess free will (thesis), which, though freely exercised over property, is limited by duty to the universal will (antithesis). The ultimate synthesis is a stage that is reached as individual will comes into harmony with universal duty. This last stage, which represents real freedom, manifests itself in the concrete institutions of the state and its laws. Hegel's view of the state (and the European nation-state in particular) as the last stage in the development of spirit and the Hegelian dialectic in general had enormous influence on late nineteenth-century nationalism, as well as on the economic theories of Karl Marx (chapter 30).

Darwin and the Theory of Evolution

Like Hegel, the British scientist Charles Darwin (d. 1882) perceived nature as constantly changing, but he surely would have challenged Hegel's opinion that "nothing new happens under the sun." A naturalist in the tradition of Aristotle, Darwin amassed enormous amounts of biological and geological data, partly as the result of a five-year trip to South America aboard the research vessel HMS *Beagle.* Darwin's study of fossils confirmed the view of his predecessors that all forms of life proceeded from earlier organic forms. The theory of evolution did not originate with Darwin—Goethe, for one, had already suggested that all forms of plant life had evolved from a single primeval plant. Darwin, however, substantiated the theory of evolution by explaining the process by which evolution occurred. Observing the tendency of organisms to increase rapidly over time and to preserve certain traits favorable to their survival, Darwin concluded that evolution operated by means of natural selection.

By natural selection, Darwin meant a process whereby nature "pruned away" unfavorable traits in a given species, permitting the survival of those creatures most suited to the struggle for life and for reproduction of their species. The elephant's trunk, the giraffe's neck, and the human brain were evidence of adjustments made by each of these species to its environment and proof that any trait that remained advantageous to a species' continuity would prevail in the species. Failure to develop such advantageous traits meant the ultimate extinction of less-developed species, in that only the "fittest" survived.

In 1859 Darwin published his classic work, *The Origin of Species by Means of Natural Selection, or the Preservation of the Favored Races in the Struggle for Life.* Less than a year later, a commentator observed, "No scientific work that has been published within this century has excited so much general curiosity." But curiosity was among the milder responses to this publication, for Darwin's law of evolution, like Newton's law of gravity, challenged traditional ideas about nature and the world order. For centuries Westerners had believed that God had supervised creation (as described in Scripture) and that human beings, created in God's image, were God's favored creatures. Darwin's theory of evolution by natural selection did not deny the idea of a divine Creator—indeed, Darwin agreed that "it is just as noble a conception of the Deity to believe that He created a few original forms capable of self-development into other and needful forms, as to believe that

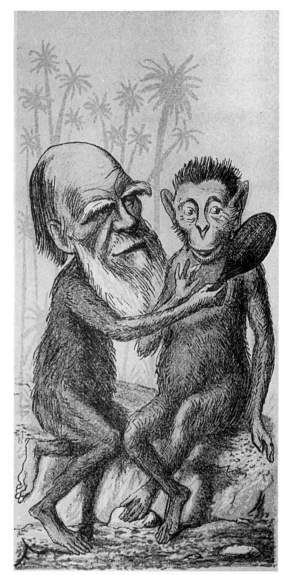

FIGURE 27.4 Spoofing evolution, a cartoon of the day portrays a simian Charles Darwin explaining his controversial theory of evolution to an ape with the help of a mirror. The work appeared in the *London Sketch Book* in May 1874, captioned by two suitable quotations from the plays of Shakespeare: "This is the ape of form" and "Four or five descents since." Archiv für Kunst Und Geschichte, Berlin.

He required a fresh act of creation to supply the voids caused by the action of His laws." But Darwin's theory implied that natural selection, not divine will, governed natural processes and that nature itself operated in random fashion. Equally troubling, the theory of evolution toppled human beings from their elevated place in the hierarchy of living creatures and suggested that all creatures were related to one another by their kinship to lower forms of life (figure 27.4). If the cosmology of Copernicus and Galileo had displaced the earth from the center of the Solar System, Darwin's theory robbed human beings of their preeminence on that planet. At a single blow, Darwin shattered the harmonious worldviews of both Renaissance humanists and Enlightenment *philosophes.*

Yet, the theory of evolution by natural selection involved a view of nature that was in keeping with romanticism, with transcendentalism, and with Asian philosophy, which presupposed an intrinsic unity of all living things. As Thoreau mused, "Am I not partly leaves and vegetable mould myself?" And numerous passages from the writings of Wordsworth, Shelley, Emerson, and Whitman exhibit a similar sort of pantheism. At the same time, Darwin's ideas encouraged an ascending "scientism" (the proposition that the methods of the natural sciences should be used in all areas of investigation) in late nineteenth-century culture (chapter 29).

The consequences of Darwin's monumental theory were far-reaching, but his ideas were often oversimplified or misinterpreted, especially by social Darwinists, who applied his theories freely to political, economic, and social life. In the context of European efforts to colonize non-Western territories, for instance, social Darwinists justified the rapacious efforts of powerful groups of people (who saw themselves as "fittest") over the less powerful. Further, the theory of evolution provided the basis for analyzing civilizations as living organisms with stages of growth, maturity, and decline. However, since Darwin meant by "fitness" the reproductive success of the species, not simply its survival, most applications of his work to social conditions represented a distortion, if not a vulgarization, of his ideas.

Beyond the impact of the theory of evolution by natural selection, Darwin's importance lay in the curiosity and intelligence he brought to his assessment of nature and the natural. Like the romantic poets, Darwin was an eager observer of nature, which he described as vast, energetic, and unceasingly dynamic. In *The Origin of Species,* he exults:

> When we no longer look at an organic being as a savage looks at a ship, as something wholly beyond his comprehension; when we regard every production of nature as one which has had a long history; when we contemplate every complex structure and instinct as the summing up of many contrivances, each useful to the possessor, in the same way as any great mechanical invention is the summing up of the labor, the experience, the reason, and even the blunders of numerous workmen; when we thus view each organic being, how far more interesting . . . does the study of natural history become!

And in the final paragraph of his opus, Darwin brings romantic fervor to his eloquent description of nature's laws:

> It is interesting to contemplate a tangled bank, clothed with many plants of many kinds, with birds singing on the bushes, with various insects flitting about, and with worms crawling through the damp earth, and to reflect that these elaborately constructed forms, so different from each other, and dependent upon each other in so complex a manner, have all been produced by laws acting around us. These laws, taken in the largest sense, being Growth and Reproduction; Inheritance which is almost implied by reproduction; Variability from the indirect and direct action of the conditions of life, and from use and disuse; a Ratio of Increase so high as to lead to a Struggle for Life, and as a consequence to Natural Selection, entailing Divergence of Character and the Extinction of less-improved forms. Thus, from the war of nature, from famine and death, the most exalted object which we are capable of conceiving, namely, the production of the higher animals, directly follows. There is grandeur in this view of life, with its several powers, having been originally breathed by the Creator into a few forms or into one; and that, whilst this planet has gone cycling on according to the fixed law of gravity, from so simple a beginning endless forms most beautiful and most wonderful have been, and are being evolved.[14]

---

[14]Charles Darwin, *The Origin of Species by Means of Natural Selection, or the Preservation of the Favored Races in the Struggle for Life,* 6th ed. (New York: Appleton, 1892), II, 280, 306.

Summary

Nature provided both a metaphor for the romantic sensibility and a refuge from the evils of nineteenth-century industrialism and urbanization. William Wordsworth, the leading nature poet of the nineteenth century, viewed the English landscape as the source of sublime inspiration and moral truth. Wordsworth and his contemporaries initiated the romantic movement in England. The romantics stressed the free exercise of the imagination, the liberation of the senses, and the cultivation of a more natural language of poetic expression. Shelley compared the elemental forces of nature with the creative powers of the poet, while Keats rejoiced that nature's fleeting beauty might forever dwell in art. American romantics endowed the quest for natural simplicity with a robust spirit of individualism. The transcendentalists Emerson and Thoreau sought a union of self with nature; Walt Whitman proclaimed his untamed and "untranslatable" ego in sympathy with nature's energy.

German philosophers, influenced by Asian philosophy and Western mysticism, saw powerful organic forces at work in nature. Hegel proposed a dialectical model according to which all reality, all history, and all ideas moved toward perfect freedom. Darwin's *Origin of the Species* theorized that species evolved into higher forms of life or failed to survive. While the theory of natural selection displaced human beings from their central place in nature, it confirmed the romantic view of the unity of nature and humankind.

GLOSSARY

dialectic   in Hegelian philosophy, the process by which every condition (or "thesis") confronts an opposite condition (or "antithesis") to resolve in synthesis

free verse   poetry that is based on irregular rhythmic patterns rather than on the conventional and regular use of meter

lyric poetry   "lyric" means accompanied by the lyre, hence, verse that is meant to be sung rather than spoken; poetry marked by individual and personal emotion (see also chapter 6)

SUGGESTIONS FOR READING

Clark, Kenneth. *Landscape into Art.* Boston: Beacon Press, 1972.

Heffernan, James A. W. *The Recreation of Landscape: A Study of Wordsworth, Coleridge, Constable and Turner.* Hanover, Mass.: University Press of New England, 1985.

Eiseley, Loren C. *Darwin's Century: Evolution and the Men Who Discovered It.* Garden City, N.J.: Doubleday, 1958.

Kroeber, Karl. *Romantic Landscape Vision: Constable and Wordsworth.* Madison: University of Wisconsin Press, 1975.

McIntish, James. *Thoreau as Romantic Naturalist: His Shifting Stance Toward Nature.* Ithaca, N.Y.: Cornell University Press, 1974.

Schwab, Raymond. *The Oriental Renaissance: Europe's Rediscovery of India and the East 1680–1880.* New York: Columbia University Press, 1984.

Schenk, H. G. *The Mind of the European Romantics.* Garden City, N.Y.: Doubleday, 1969.

Wordsworth, Jonathan, and others. *William Wordsworth and the Age of English Romanticism.* New Brunswick, N.J.: Rutgers University Press, 1989.

28

THE ROMANTIC HERO

As the romantics idealized nature and the natural, so they exalted the creative singularity of the individual in the person of the hero. Heroes, whether mortal or semidivine, traditionally symbolized humanity at its best, most powerful, and most godlike. The heroes of such classics as the *Epic of Gilgamesh,* the *Mahabharata,* the *Iliad,* the *Aeneid,* the *Song of Roland,* and *Sundiata* were larger-than-life figures with extraordinary expectations, abilities, and goals. The heroes of old embodied the shared values of the culture they represented. Likewise, the romantic hero was a figure of superhuman ambitions and extraordinary achievements. But romantic heroes differed from traditional literary heroes in that they tended to challenge rather than champion the social and moral values of their time. Egocentric and occasionally misanthropic, the heroes of the romantic era were unique personalities, rarely communal symbols. Among the most notable heroes of the era were its artists. Fascinated by European folklore, medieval legend, and Asian customs, romantic artists modeled themselves after the heroes of "exotic" cultures. They passionately defended the notion that artists both create and are created by their art.

Nineteenth-century intellectuals were fascinated by the nature of the heroic personality. The prose essays of Ralph Waldo Emerson (chapter 27) described the hero as the ultimate individual, and, in 1841, the British historian and essayist Thomas Carlyle (d. 1881) published a series of lectures, *On Heroes and Hero-Worship,* in which he glorified hero-gods, prophets, poets, priests, men of letters, and the quasi-legendary Napoleon Bonaparte. Walter Scott (d. 1832) and Alexandre Dumas (d. 1825) wrote historical novels that described the heroic adventures of swashbuckling soldiers and maidens in distress, while Victor Hugo (d. 1825) produced such novels as *Les Misérables,* which made sentimental heroes out of egalitarian patriots. In America, too, the hero occupied the attention of artists: the novelists Nathaniel Hawthorne (d. 1864) and Herman Melville (d. 1891) created brooding, melancholic heroes whose moral strength was tested by the forces of evil.

The nineteenth century did not produce more heroes than other centuries, but it visibly exalted heroic achievement and glorified the role of the heroic

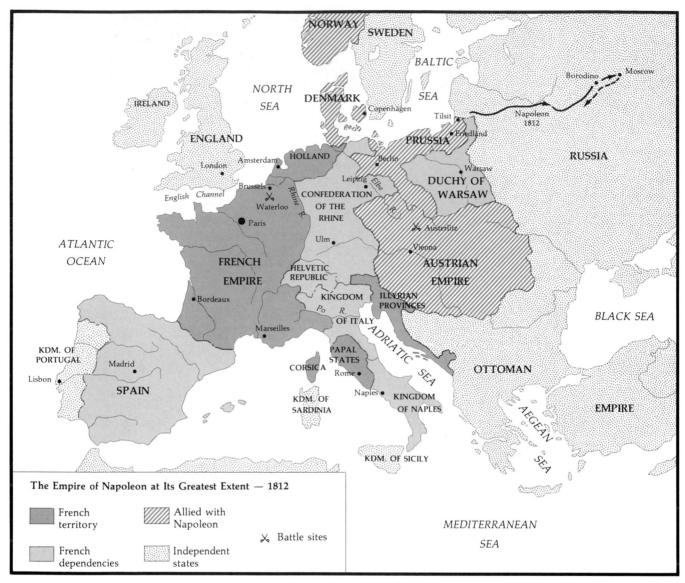

MAP 28.1 Napoleonic Europe, 1815.

imagination. While Enlightenment writers studied the social animal, the romantics explored the depths of their own souls. With a subjectivity bordering on egotism, the romantics saw *themselves* as heroes—the champions of a cult of the senses and of the heart. They eagerly embraced all means of heightening imaginative experience, including those induced by such hallucinogens as opium. "*Exister, pour nous, c'est sentir*" ("For us, to exist is to feel"), Rousseau had proclaimed in the late eighteenth century. And, on the first page of his *Confessions,* the prophet of romanticism anticipated the sentiments of self-conscious individualism that would drive artists of the next two generations: "I am made unlike any one I have ever met: I will even venture to say that I am like no one in the whole world. I may be no better, but at least I am different."

Napoleon as a Romantic Hero

In 1799 the thirty-year-old Napoleon Bonaparte (d. 1821) seized control of the government of France. "The Revolution is ended," announced the Corsican army general when he proclaimed himself emperor in 1804. In the following ten years, Napoleon pursued a brilliant policy of conquest that brought all of Western Europe to his feet. Throughout much of the West Napoleon abolished serfdom, expropriated Church possessions, curtailed feudal privileges, and introduced French laws, institutions, and influence. Napoleon spread the revolutionary ideals of liberty, fraternity, and equality throughout the empire (Map 28.1). He championed popular sovereignty and kindled the sentiments of nationalism. In France, Napoleon ended civil strife, reorganized the educational system, and institutionalized the system of civil law known as the *Code Napoléon.*

FIGURE 28.1 *Napoleon Crossing the Great Saint Bernard Pass,* Jacques-Louis David, 1800. Oil on canvas, 8 ft. 8 in. × 7 ft. 7 in. Kunsthistorishe Museum, Vienna.

If Napoleon's ambitions were heroic, his military campaigns were stunning. Having conquered Italy, Egypt, Austria, Prussia, Portugal, and Spain, he pressed on to Russia, where , in 1812, bitter weather and lack of food forced his armies to retreat. Only 100,000 of his army of 600,000 survived. In 1813, a coalition of European powers forced his defeat and exile to the island of Elba off the coast of Italy. A second and final defeat occurred after he escaped in 1814, raised a new army, and met the combined European forces led by the English duke of Wellington at the battle of Waterloo. The fallen hero spent the last years of his life in exile on the barren island of Saint Helena off the west coast of Africa.

Napoleon, the first of the modern European dictators, left a distinctly neoclassical stamp upon the city of Paris (chapter 26). However, with the help of David, his favorite artist, he became the nineteenth century's first romantic hero (figure 28.1). Although his deeds were his greatest achievement, his ideas, as expressed in his diary, were equally significant. The diary—an intimate record of personal reflections and feelings—became a favorite mode of expression for such nineteenth-century romantics as Delacroix, Beethoven, George Sand, and Mary Shelley. Napoleon's diary entries of 1800, 1802, and 1817, quoted in Reading 100, reveal some of the typical features of the romantic personality: self-conscious individualism, a sense of personal power, unbridled egotism, and a high regard for the life of the imagination.

Milan, June 17, 1800: . . . What a thing is imagination! Here are men who don't know me, who have never seen me, but who only knew of me, and they are moved by my presence, they would do anything for me! And this same incident arises in all centuries and in all countries! Such is fanaticism! Yes, imagination rules the world. The defect of our modern institutions is that they do not speak to the imagination. By that alone can man be governed; without it he is but a brute.

December 30, 1802: My power proceeds from my reputation, and my reputation from the victories I have won. My power would fall if I were not to support it with more glory and more victories. Conquest has made me what I am; only conquest can maintain me . . . .

Saint Helena, March 3, 1817: In spite of all the libels, I have no fear whatever about my fame. Posterity will do me justice. The truth will be known; and the good I have done will be compared with the faults I have committed. I am not uneasy as to the result. Had I succeeded, I would have died with the reputation of the greatest man that ever existed. As it is, although I have failed, I shall be considered as an extraordinary man: my elevation was unparalleled, because unaccompanied by crime. I have fought fifty pitched battles, almost all of which I have won. I have framed and carried into effect a code of laws that will bear my name to the most distant posterity. I raised myself from nothing to be the most powerful monarch in the world. Europe was at my feet. I have always been of [the] opinion that the sovereignty lay in the people.

The Promethean Hero

If Napoleon was nineteenth-century Europe's favorite real-life hero, Prometheus was its favorite fictional hero. Prometheus (the name means "forethought") was one of the primordial deities of Greek mythology. According to Greek legend, he stole from Mount Olympus—the home of the gods—the sacred fire, by which he civilized humankind. To punish Prometheus for this arrogant act (and also for having concealed his foreknowledge of Zeus' downfall), Zeus chained him to a lonely rock, where a vulture fed daily on his liver. A second, less dramatic, aspect of the Prometheus story, more popular among the Romans than the Greeks, credited Prometheus with having fashioned human beings out of clay, in the manner of the Babylonian hero-god Marduk (chapter 2).

Romantic poets embraced the figure of Prometheus as the suffering champion of humanity—a deliverer and a creator whose noble ambitions had incurred the wrath of the gods. Percy Bysshe Shelley, whom we met in chapter 27, made Prometheus the savior-hero of his four-act drama *Prometheus Unbound.* In the drama, Prometheus frees the universe from the tyranny of the gods. Mary Godwin Shelley (Shelley's second wife and the daughter of William Godwin and the feminist writer Mary Wollstonecraft) explored the second aspect of the legend, that of Prometheus as creator, in her novel *Frankenstein; or, The Modern Prometheus.* In this classic work, the Promethean scientist Victor Frankenstein creates a monster who, like a fallen Lucifer, becomes a symbol of heroic evil. Ironically, the monster, rather than the scientist, captured the modern imagination, even to the point of usurping the name of his creator.

The Promethean myth found its most passionate champion in the life and works of the British poet George Gordon, Lord Byron (d. 1824). Byron was one of the most flamboyant personalities of the age (figure 28.2). Dedicated to the pleasures of the senses, he was equally impassioned by the ideals of liberty and brotherhood. In his brief, mercurial life, he established the prototype of the romantic hero, often called—after Byron himself—the Byronic hero. As a young man, Byron traveled restlessly throughout Europe and the Mediterranean, devouring the landscape and the major sites. A physically attractive man (despite the handicap of a club foot) with dark, brooding eyes, he engaged in numerous love affairs, including one with his half-sister, a union that produced an illegitimate daughter. In 1816, Byron abandoned an unsuccessful marriage and left England for good. He lived in Italy for a time with the Shelleys and a string of mistresses before sailing to Greece, where he died while defending the cause of Greek independence from the Turks.

Throughout his life, Byron was given to periodic bouts of creativity and dissipation. A man of violent passions, he harbored a desperate need to unbosom his innermost thoughts and feelings. In Italy, where he composed two of his greatest poems, *Childe Harold's Pilgrimage* and *Don Juan,* he described his frenzied spirit thus: "half mad . . . between metaphysics, mountains, lakes, love unextinguishable, thoughts unutterable, and the nightmare of my own delinquencies." The heroes of Byron's poems were surely autobiographical: Childe Harold, the wanderer who, alienated from society, seeks companionship in nature; Don Juan, the libertine who cannot satiate his sexual desires; and Prometheus, the god who "stole from Heaven the flame, for which he fell." Prometheus preoccupied Byron as a symbol of triumphant individualism. For Byron, capturing the imagination in art or in life was comparable to stealing the sacred fire. In a number of his poems, Byron compared the fallen Napoleon to the mythic Prometheus—symbol

FIGURE 28.2 *Lord Byron 6th Baron in Albanian Costume,* Thomas Phillips, 1813. Oil on canvas, 29 1/2 in. × 24 1/2 in. National Portrait Gallery, London.

of heroic ambition and ungovernable passions. And, in the stirring ode called simply "Prometheus" (1816), Byron made of the Promethean myth a parable for the romantic imagination. He begins by recalling the traditional story of the hero whose "Godlike crime was to be kind." He goes on to identify Prometheus as "a symbol and a sign" to mortals who, also "part divine," anticipate their "funereal destiny" but who, like Prometheus, must strive to defy that destiny. Byron's verses mingle defiance and hope with melancholy and despair.

READING 101 Byron's "Prometheus"

Titan! to whose immortal eyes   1
    The sufferings of mortality,
    Seen in their sad reality,
Were not as things that gods despise;
What was thy pity's recompense?
A silent suffering, and intense;
The rock,the vulture, and the chain,
All that the proud can feel of pain,
The agony they do not show,
The suffocating sense of woe,   10
    Which speaks but in its loneliness,
And then is jealous lest the sky
Should have a listener, nor will sigh
    Until its voice is echoless.

Titan! to thee the strife was given
    Between the suffering and the will,
    Which torture where they cannot kill;
And the inexorable Heaven,
And the deaf tyranny of Fate,
The ruling principle of Hate,   20
Which for its pleasure doth create
The things it may annihilate,
Refused thee even the boon to die:
The wretched gift eternity
Was thine—and thou hast borne it well.
All that the Thunderer[1] wrung from thee
Was but the menace which flung back
On him the torments of thy rack;
The fate thou didst so well foresee,
But would not to appease him tell;   30
And in thy Silence was his Sentence,
And in his Soul a vain repentance,
And evil dread so ill dissembled,
That in his hand the lightnings trembled.

Thy Godlike crime was to be kind,
    To render with thy precepts less
    The sum of human wretchedness,
And strengthen Man with his own mind;
But baffled as thou wert from high,
Still in thy patient energy,   40
In the endurance, and repulse
    Of thine impenetrable Spirit,
Which Earth and Heaven could not convulse,
    A mightly lesson we inherit:
Thou art a symbol and a sign
    To Mortals of their fate and force;
Like thee, Man is in part divine,
    A troubled stream from a pure source;
And Man in portions can foresee
His own funereal destiny,   50
His wretchedness, and his resistance,
And his sad unallied existence:
To which his Spirit may oppose
Itself—and equal to all woes,
    And a firm will, and a deep sense,
Which even in torture can descry
    Its own concenter'd recompense,[2]
Triumphant where it dares defy,
And making Death a Victory.

---

[1]Zeus, the supreme god of the Greeks.
[2]Catch a glimpse of the Spirit's own sufficient reward.

Goethe's Faust: The Quintessential Romantic Hero

Of all literary heroes of the nineteenth century, perhaps the most compelling was Doctor Faustus. The original Johann or Georg Faust, a character whose origins are found in sixteenth-century legend, seems to have been a traveling physician and a practitioner of black magic. Reputed to have sold his soul to the devil in exchange for infinite knowledge and personal experience, he became the subject of a tragedy by Shakespeare's contemporary, Christopher Marlowe, as well as the inspiration for a number of popular stories and puppet plays. Faust was the favorite Renaissance symbol of the human lust for knowledge and experience balanced against the perils of eternal damnation, a motif that figured largely in literary characterizations of Don Juan as well. To nineteenth-century poets, however, Faust was the quintessential romantic hero, the symbol of the human desire to transcend physical limitations and to master all realms of knowledge. The Faustian hero—like Prometheus or the apotheosized Napoleon—sought power that might permit him to control the world. In the hands of the German poet Johann Wolfgang von Goethe (d. 1832), Faust became the paradigm of Western man and—more broadly—of the human quest for knowledge, experience, and power.

Goethe's *Faust* is one of the most monumental literary works of its time. Goethe conceived the piece during the 1770s, began writing in 1808, and completed it more than twenty years later; hence, *Faust* was the product of Goethe's entire career. Although ostensibly a drama, *Faust* more closely resembles an epic poem. It is written in a lyric German, with a freedom of rhyme and meter that is typical of romantic poetry. As a play, it deliberately ignores the classical unities of time and place—indeed, its shifting, "cinematic" qualities make it more adaptable to modern film than to the traditional stage. Despite a cosmic breadth that compares with Milton's *Paradise Lost* or Dante's *Divine Comedy,* Goethe's *Faust* focuses more narrowly on the human condition. Goethe neither seeks to justify God's ways to humanity nor to allegorize the Christian ascent to salvation; rather, he uncovers the tragic tension between heroic aspirations and human limitations. Goethe, a student of law, medicine, theology, theater, biology, optics, and alchemy, seems to have modeled Faust after himself: Faust is a man of deep learning, a Christian, and a scientist. He is, moreover, a creative genius whose desire to know and achieve has dominated his life. But he feels stale, bored, and deeply dissatisfied with all theoretical modes of understanding. He is driven to exhaust other kinds of experience—not only intellectual but sensual, erotic, aesthetic, and, finally, spiritual.

The Prologue of *Faust* is set in Heaven, where (in a manner reminiscent of the Book of Job), a wager is made between Mephistopheles (Satan) and God. Mephistopheles bets God that he can divert Faust from "the path that is true and fit." God contends that though "men make mistakes as long as they strive," Faust will never relinquish his soul to Satan. In the first part of the tragedy, Mephistopheles proceeds to make a second pact, this one with Faust himself: if he can satisfy Faust's deepest desires and ambitions to the point of the hero's satisfaction, then Mephistopheles will win Faust's soul. Mephistopheles lures the despairing Faust out of the study that Faust calls "This God-damned dreary hole in the wall"—away from the life of the mind and into the larger world of experience (figure 28.3). The hero then engages in a passionate love affair with a young maiden named Gretchen. Discovering the joys of the sensual life, Faust proclaims the priority of the heart ("Feeling is all!") over the mind. Faust's romance, however, has tragic consequences, including the death of Gretchen's mother, child, brother, and, ultimately, Gretchen herself. Nevertheless, Gretchen's pure and selfless love wins her salvation.

In the second part of Goethe's *Faust,* and symbolically, in the life of Faust's imagination—the hero travels with Mephistopheles through a netherworld in which he meets an array of witches, sirens, and other fantastic creatures. He also encounters the ravishing Helen of Troy. Helen, the symbol of ideal beauty, acquaints Faust with the entire history and culture of humankind; but Faust remains unsated. His unquenched thirst for experience now leads him to pursue a life of action for the public good: he undertakes a vast land-reclamation project that provides habitation for millions of people. And in this endeavor—so different, it might be observed, from Candide's reclusive "garden"—the aged and near-blind Faust begins to find personal fulfillment. He dies, however, before fully realizing his dream; hence he never actually avows the satisfaction that would send his soul to Hell. And although Mephistopheles gathers a hellish host to apprehend Faust's soul when it leaves his body, God's angels spirit his soul to Heaven.

The heroic Faust is a timeless symbol of the Western drive for consummate knowledge, experience, and the will to power over nature. Though it is possible to reproduce here only a small portion of Goethe's twelve-thousand-line poem, the following excerpt conveys the powerful lyricism, the verbal subtleties, and the shifts between high seriousness and comedy that make Goethe's *Faust* a literary masterpiece.

Mepß : Pourquoi tout ce vacarme ? que demande Monsieur ? qu'y a-t-il pour son service ?

FIGURE 28.3 *Mephistopheles Appearing to Faust in his Study,* Illustration for Goethe's *Faust,* Eugène Delacroix, 1828. Lithograph, 10 3/4 in. × 9 in. The Metropolitan Museum of Art, Rogers Fund, New York City, 1917 (17.12).

READING 102 From Goethe's *Faust*

Prologue in Heaven
The Lord. The Heavenly Hosts. Mephistopheles following (The Three Archangels step forward)

Raphael: The chanting sun, as ever, rivals
The chanting of his brother spheres
And marches round his destined circuit—[3]
A march that thunders in our ears.
His aspect cheers the Hosts of Heaven
Though what his essence none can say;
These inconceivable creations
Keep the high state of their first day.

---

[3]The sun is treated here as one of the planets, all of which, according to Pythagoras, moved harmoniously in crystalline spheres.

Gabriel: And swift, with inconceivable swiftness,
The earth's full splendor rolls around,   10
Celestial radiance alternating
With a dread night too deep to sound;
The sea against the rocks' deep bases
Comes foaming up in far-flung force,
And rock and sea go whirling onward
In the swift spheres' eternal course.

Michael: And storms in rivalry are raging
From sea to land, from land to sea,
In frenzy forge the world a girdle
From which no inmost part is free.   20
The blight of lightning flaming yonder
Marks where the thunder-bolt will play;
And yet Thine envoys, Lord, revere
The gentle movement of Thy day.

Choir of Angels: Thine aspect cheers the Hosts of Heaven
Though what Thine essence none can say,
And all Thy loftiest creations
Keep the high state of their first day.

(Enter Mephistopheles)[4]

Mephistopheles: Since you, O Lord, once more approach and ask
If business down with us be light or heavy—   30

And in the past you've usually welcomed me—
That's why you see me also at your levee.
Excuse me, I can't manage lofty words—
Not though your whole court jeer and find me low;
My pathos certainly would make you laugh
Had you not left off laughing long ago.
Your suns and worlds mean nothing much to me;
How men torment themselves, that's all I see.
The little god of the world, one can't reshape, reshade him;
He is as strange to-day as that first day you made him.   40
His life would be not so bad, not quite,
Had you not granted him a gleam of Heaven's light;
He calls it Reason, uses it not the least
Except to be more beastly than any beast.
He seems to me—if your Honor does not mind—
Like a grasshopper—the long-legged kind—
That's always in flight and leaps as it flies along
And then in the grass strikes up its same old song.
I could only wish he confined himself to the grass!
He thrusts his nose into every filth, alas.   50
    Lord: Mephistopheles, have you no other news?
Do you always come here to accuse?
Is nothing ever right in your eyes on earth?
    Mephistopheles: No, Lord! I find things there as downright bad as ever.
I am sorry for men's days of dread and dearth;
Poor things, *my* wish to plague 'em isn't fervent.
    Lord: Do you know Faust?
    Mephistopheles: The Doctor?
    Lord: Aye, my servant.[5]
    Mephistopheles: Indeed! He serves you oddly   60
enough, I think.
The fool has no earthly habits in meat and drink.
The ferment in him drives him wide and far,
That he is mad he too has almost guessed;
He demands of heaven each fairest star
And of earth each highest joy and best,
And all that is new and all that is far
Can bring no calm to the deep-sea swell of his breast.
    Lord: Now he may serve me only gropingly,
Soon I shall lead him into the light.
The gardener knows when the sapling first turns green   70
That flowers and fruit will make the future bright.

Mephistopheles: What do you wager? You will lose him yet,
Provided *you* give *me* permission
To steer him gently the course I set.
    Lord: So long as he walks the earth alive,
So long you may try what enters your head;
Men make mistake as long as they strive.
    Mephistopheles: I thank you for that; as regards the dead,
The dead have never taken my fancy.
I favor cheeks that are full and rosy-red;   80
No corpse is welcome to my house;
I work as the cat does with the mouse.
    Lord: Very well; you have my full permission.
Divert this soul from its primal source
And carry it, if you can seize it,
Down with you upon your course—
And stand ashamed when you must needs admit:
A good man with his groping intuitions
Still knows the path that true and fit.
    Mephistopheles: All right—but it won't last for   90
long.
I'm not afraid my bet will turn out wrong.
And, if my aim prove true and strong,
Allow me to triumph wholeheartedly.
Dust shall he eat—and greedily—
Like my cousin the Snake renowned in tale and song.[6]
    Lord: That too you are free to give a trial;
I have never hated the likes of you.
Of all the spirits of denial
The joker is the last that I eschew.
Man finds relaxation too attractive—   100
Too fond too soon of unconditional rest;
Which is why I am pleased to give him a companion
Who lures and thrusts and must, as devil, be active.
But ye, true sons of Heaven,[7] it is your duty
To take your joy in the living wealth of beauty.
The changing Essence which ever works and lives
Wall you around with love, serene, secure!
And that which floats in flickering appearance
Fix ye it firm in thoughts that must endure.
    Choir of Angels: Thine aspect cheers the Hosts of   110
Heaven
Though what Thine essence none can say,
And all Thy loftiest creations
Keep the high state of their first day.

(Heaven closes)

Mephistopheles (*alone*): I like to see the Old One now and then
And try to keep relations on the level.
It's really decent of so great a person
To talk so humanely even to the Devil.

---

[4]The name possibly derives from the Hebrew "Mephistoph," meaning "destroyer of the gods."
[5]Compare the exchange between God and Satan at the beginning of the Book of Job. (Reading 4D).

[6]In Genesis 3:14, Satan condemns the serpent to go on its belly and eat dust for the rest of its days.
[7]The archangels.

The First Part of the Tragedy

Night

(In a high-vaulted narrow Gothic room Faust, restless, in a chair at his desk)

Faust: Here stand I, ach, Philosophy
Behind me and Law and Medicine too
And, to my cost, Theology—[8]   120
All these I have sweated through and through
And now you see me a poor fool
As wise as when I entered school!
They call me Master, they call me Doctor,[9]
Ten years now I have dragged my college
Along by the nose through zig and zag
Through up and down and round and round
And this is all that I have found—
The impossibility of knowledge!
It is this that burns away my heart;   130
Of course I am cleverer than the quacks,
Than master and doctor, than clerk and priest,
I suffer no scruple or doubt in the least,
I have no qualms about devil or burning,
Which is just why all joy is torn from me,
I cannot presume to make use of my learning,
I cannot presume I could open my mind
To proselytize and improve mankind.

Besides, I have neither goods nor gold,
Neither reputation nor rank in the world;   140
No dog would choose to continue so!
Which is why I have given myself to Magic
To see if the Spirit may grant me to know
Through its force and its voice full many a secret,
May spare the sour sweat that I used to pour out
In talking of what I know nothing about,
May grant me to learn what it is that girds
The world together in its inmost being,
That the seeing its whole germination, the seeing
Its workings, may end my traffic in words.   150

O couldst thou, light of the full moon,
Look now thy last upon my pain,
Thou for whom I have sat belated
So many midnights here and waited
Till, over books and papers, thou
Didst shine, sad friend, upon my brow!
O could I but walk to and fro
On mountain heights in thy dear glow
Or float with spirits round mountain eyries
Or weave through fields thy glances glean   160
And freed from all miasmal theories
Bathe in thy dew and wash me clean![10]

Oh! Am I still stuck in this jail?
This God-damned dreary hole in the wall
Where even the lovely light of heaven
Breaks wanly through the painted panes!
Cooped up among these heaps of books
Gnawed by worms, coated with dust,
Round which to the top of the Gothic vault
A smoke-stained paper forms a crust.   170
Retorts and canisters lie pell-mell
And pyramids of instruments,
The junk of centuries, dense and mat—
Your world, man! World? They call it that!

And yet you ask why your poor heart
Cramped in your breast should feel such fear,
Why an unspecified misery
Should throw your life so out of gear?
Instead of the living natural world
For which God made all men his sons   180
You hold a reeking mouldering court
Among assorted skeletons.
Away! There is a world outside!
And this one book of mystic art
Which Nostradamus[11] wrote himself,
Is this not adequate guard and guide?
By this you can tell the course of the stars,
By this, once Nature gives the word,
The soul begins to stir and dawn,
A spirit by a spirit heard.   190
In vain your barren studies here
Construe the signs of sanctity.
You Spirits, you are hovering near;
If you can hear me, answer me!

(He opens the book and perceives the sign of the Macrocosm)[12]

Ha! What a river of wonder at this vision
Bursts upon all my senses in one flood!
And I feel young, the holy joy of life
Glows new, flows fresh, through nerve and blood!
Was it a god designed this hieroglyph to calm
The storm which but now raged inside me,   200
To pour upon my heart such balm,
And by some secret urge to guide me
Where all the powers of Nature stand unveiled around
   me?
Am I a God? It grows so light!
And through the clear-cut symbol on this page
My soul comes face to face with all creating Nature.
At last I understand the dictum of the sage:
'The spiritual world is always open,
Your mind is closed, your heart is dead;
Rise, young man, and plunge undaunted   210
Your earthly breast in the mourning red.'

---

[8]Philosophy, law, medicine, and theology were the four programs of study in medieval universities.
[9]The two advanced degrees beyond the baccalaureate.
[10]Goethe's conception of nature as a source of sublime purification may be compared with similar ideas held by the nature poets and the transcendentalists discussed in chapter 27.

---

[11]Michel de Notredame or Nostradamus (d. 1566) was a French astrologer famous for his prophecies of future events.
[12]Signs of the universe, such as the pentagram, were especially popular among those who practiced magic and the occult arts.

(He contemplates the sign)

Into one Whole how all things blend,
Function and live within each other!
Passing gold buckets to each other
How heavenly powers ascend, descend!
The odor of grace upon their wings,
They thrust from heaven through earthly things
And as all sing so *the* All sings!
What a fine show! Aye, but only a show!
Infinite Nature, where can I tap thy veins?   220

Where are thy breasts, those well-springs of all life
On which hang heaven and earth,
Towards which my dry breast strains?
They well up, they give drink, but I feel drought and
    dearth.

*(He turns the pages and perceives the sign of the Earth
Spirit)*[13]

How differently this new sign works upon me!
Thy sign, thou Spirit of the Earth, 'tis thine
And thou art nearer to me.
At once I feel my powers unfurled,
At once I glow as from new wine
And feel inspired to venture into the world,   230
To cope with the fortunes of earth benign or malign,
To enter the ring with the storm, to grapple and clinch,
To enter the jaws of the shipwreck and never flinch.
Over me comes a mist,
The moon muffles her light,
The lamp goes dark.
The air goes damp. Red beams flash
Around my head. There blows
A kind of a shudder down from the vault
And seizes on me.   240
It is thou must be hovering round me, come at my
    prayers!
Spirit, unveil thyself!
My heart, oh my heart, how it tears!
And how each and all of my senses
Seem burrowing upwards towards new light, new
    breath!
I feel my heart has surrendered, I have no more
    defences.
Come then! Come! Even if it prove my death!

*(He seizes the book and solemnly pronounces the sign
of the Earth Spirit. There is a flash of red flame and the
Spirit appears in it)*

Spirit: Who calls upon me?
Faust: Appalling vision!
Spirit: You have long been sucking at my sphere,   250
Now by main force you have drawn me here
And now—

---

[13]The Earth Spirit, here used to represent the active, sensual side of
Faust's nature as opposed to the contemplative, spiritual side represented
by the Macrocosm. Goethe suggested representing the *Erdgeist* on the
stage by means of a magic lantern device that would magnify and project
the head of Apollo or Zeus at giant proportions.

Faust: No! Not to be endured!
Spirit: With prayers and with pantings you have
    procured
The sight of my face and the sound of my voice—
Now I am here. What a pitiable shivering
Seizes the Superman. Where is the call of your soul?
Where the breast which created a world in itself
And carried and fostered it, swelling up, joyfully
    quivering,
Raising itself to a level with Us, the Spirits?   260
Where are you, Faust, whose voice rang out to me,
Who with every nerve so thrust yourself upon me?
Are you the thing that at a whiff of my breath
Trembles throughout its living frame,
A poor worm crawling off, askance, askew?
Faust: Shall I yield to Thee, Thou shape of flame?
I am Faust, I can hold my own with Thee.
Spirit: In the floods of life, in the storm of work,
In ebb and flow,
In warp and weft,   270
Cradle and grave,
An eternal sea,
A changing patchwork,
A glowing life,
At the whirring loom of Time I weave
The living clothes of the Deity.
Faust: Thou who dost rove the wide world round,
Busy Spirit, how near I feel to Thee!
Spirit: You are like that Spirit which you can grasp,
Not me!   280

(The Spirit vanishes)

Faust: Not Thee!
Whom then?
I who am Godhead's image,
Am I not even like Thee!

(A knocking on the door)

Death! I know who that is. My assistant!
So ends my happiest, fairest hour.
The crawling pedant must interrupt
My visions at their fullest flower!

[*Faust converses with his assistant Wagner on the
fruitlessness of a life of study. When Wagner leaves,
Faust prepares to commit suicide; but he is interrupted
by the sounds of churchbells and choral music. Still
brooding, he joins Wagner and the townspeople as they
celebrate Easter Sunday. At the city gate, Faust
encounters a black poodle, which he takes back with
him to his studio. The dog is actually Mephistopheles,
who soon makes his real self known to Faust.*]

(The same room. Later)

Faust: Who's knocking? Come in! *Now* who wants
to annoy me?
Mephistopheles:(*outside door*): It's I.   290
Faust: Come in!
Mephistopheles:(*outside door*): You must say
'Come in' three times.

Faust: Come in then!
Mephistopheles: *(entering)*: Thank you; you
    overjoy me.
We two, I hope, we shall be good friends;
To chase those megrims[14] of yours away
I am here like a fine young squire to-day,
In a suit of scarlet trimmed with gold
And a little cape of stiff brocade,
With a cock's feather in my hat   300
And at my side a long sharp blade,
And the most succinct advice I can give
Is that you dress up just like me,
So that uninhibited and free
You may find out what is means to live.
    Faust: The pain of earth's constricted life, I fancy,
Will pierce me still, whatever my attire;
I am too old for mere amusement,
Too young to be without desire.
How can the world dispel my doubt?   310
You must do without, you must do without!
That is the everlasting song
Which rings in every ear, which rings,
And which to us our whole life long
Every hour hoarsely sings.
I wake in the morning only to feel appalled,
My eyes with bitter tears could run
To see the day which in its course
Will not fulfil a wish for me, not one';
The day which whittles away with obstinate carping   320
All pleasures—even those of anticipation,
Which makes a thousand grimaces to obstruct
My heart when it is stirring in creation.
And again, when night comes down, in anguish
I must stretch out upon my bed
And again no rest is granted me,
For wild dreams fill my mind with dread.
The God who dwells within my bosom
Can make my inmost soul react;
The God who sways my every power   330
Is powerless with external fact.
And so existence weighs upon my breast
And I long for death and life—life I detest.
    Mephistopheles: Yet death is never a wholly
    welcome guest.
    Faust: O happy is he whom death in the dazzle of
    victory
Crowns with the bloody laurel in the battling swirl!
Or he whom after the mad and breakneck dance
He comes upon in the arms of a girl!
O to have sunk away, delighted, deleted,
Before the Spirit of the Earth,[15] before his might!   340
    Mephistopheles: Yet I know someone who failed to
    drink
A brown juice on a certain night.[16]
    Faust: Your hobby is espionage—is it not?
    Mephistopheles: Oh I'm not omniscient—but I
    know a lot.

    Faust: Whereas that tumult in my soul
Was stilled by sweet familiar chimes
Which cozened the child that yet was in me
With echoes of more happy times,
I now curse all things that encompass
The soul with lures and jugglery   350
And bind it in this dungeon of grief
With trickery and flattery.
Cursed in advance be the high opinion
That serves our spirit for a cloak!
Cursed be the dazzle of appearance
Which bows our senses to its yoke!
Cursed be the lying dreams of glory,
The illusion that our name survives!
Cursed be the flattering things we own,
Servants and ploughs, children and wives!   360
Cursed be Mammon[17] when with his treasures
He makes us play the adventurous man
Or when for our luxurious pleasures
He duly spreads the soft divan!
A curse on the balsam of the grape!
A curse on the love that rides for a fall!
A curse on hope! A curse on faith!
And a curse on patience most of all!

(The invisible Spirits sing again)

    Spirits: Woe! Woe!
You have destroyed it,   370
The beautiful world;
By your violent hand
'Tis downward hurled!
A half-god has dashed it asunder!
From under
We bear off the rubble to nowhere
And ponder
Sadly the beauty departed.
Magnipotent
One among men,   380
Magnificent
Build it again,
Build it again in your breast!
Let a new course of life
Begin
With vision abounding
And new songs resounding
To welcome it in!
    Mephistopheles: These are the juniors
Of my faction.   390
Hear how precociously they counsel
Pleasure and action.
Out and away
From your lonely day
Which dries your senses and your juices
Their melody seduces.
Stop playing with your grief which battens
Like a vulture on your life, your mind!

---

[14]Low or morbid spirits.
[15]The Earth Spirit of the previous passage.
[16]Mephistopheles alludes to Faust's contemplation of suicide by poison earlier in the drama.

---

[17]Riches or material wealth.

The worst of company would make you feel
That you are a man among mankind.   400
Not that it's really my proposition
To shove you among the common men;
Though I'm not one of the Upper Ten,
If you would like a coalition
With me for your career through life,
I am quite ready to fit in,
I'm yours before you can say knife.
I am your comrade;
If you so crave,
I am your servant, I am your slave.   410

    Faust: And what have I to undertake in return?

    Mephistopheles: Oh it's early days to discuss what
that is.

    Faust: No, no, the devil is an egoist
And ready to do nothing gratis
Which is to benefit a stranger.
Tell me your terms and don't prevaricate!
A servant like you in the house is a danger.

    Mephistopheles: I will bind myself to your service
in this world,
To be at your beck and never rest nor slack;
When we meet again on the other side,   420
In the same coin you shall pay me back.

    Faust: The other side gives me little trouble;
First batter this present world to rubble,
Then the other may rise—if that's the plan.
This earth is where my springs of joy have started,
And this sun shines on me when broken-hearted;
If I can first from them be parted,
Then let happen what will and can!
I wish to hear no more about it—
Whether there too men hate and love   430
Or whether in those spheres too, in the future,
There is a Below or an Above.

    Mephistopheles: With such an outlook you can
risk it.
Sign on the line! In these next days you will get
Ravishing samples of my arts;
I am giving you what never man saw yet.

    Faust: Poor devil, can *you* give anything ever?
Was a human spirit in its high endeavor
Even once understood by one of your breed?
Have you got food which fails to feed?   440
Or red gold which, never at rest,
Like mercury runs away through the hand?
A game at which one never wins?
A girl who, even when on my breast,
Pledges herself to my neighbor with her eyes?
The divine and lovely delight of honor
Which falls like a falling star and dies?
Show me the fruits which, before they are plucked,
    decay
And the trees which day after day renew their green!

    Mephistopheles: Such a commission doesn't   450
alarm me,
I have such treasures to purvey.
But, my good friend, the time draws on when we
Should be glad to feast at our ease on something good.

    Faust: If ever I stretch myself on a bed of ease,
Then I am finished! Is that understood?
If ever your flatteries can coax me
To be pleased with myself, if ever you cast
A spell of pleasure that can hoax me—
Then let *that* day be my last!
That's my wager![18]   460

    Mephistopheles: Done!

    Faust: Let's shake!
If ever I say to the passing moment
'Linger a while! Thou art so fair!'
Then you may cast me into fetters,
I will gladly perish then and there!
Then you may set the death-bell tolling,
Then from my service you are free,
The clock may stop, its hand may fall,
And that be the end of time for me!   470

    Mephistopheles: Think what you're saying, we
shall not forget it.

    Faust: And you are fully within your rights;
I have made no mad or outrageous claim.
If I stay as I am, I am a slave—
Whether yours or another's, it's all the same.

    Mephistopheles: I shall this very day at the College
Banquet
Enter your service with no more ado,
But just one point—As a life-and-death insurance
I must trouble you for a line or two.

    Faust: So you, you pedant, you too like things in   480
writing?
Have you never known a man? Or a man's word?
Never?
Is it not enough that my word of mouth
Puts all my days in bond for ever?
Does not the world rage on in all its streams
And shall a promise hamper *me*?
Yet this illusion reigns within our hearts
And from it who would be gladly free?
Happy the man who can inwardly keep his word;
Whatever the cost, he will not be loath to pay!   490
But a parchment, duly inscribed and sealed,
Is a bogey from which all wince away.
The word dies on the tip of the pen
And wax and leather lord it then.
What do you, evil spirit, require?
Bronze, marble, parchment, paper?
Quill or chisel or pencil of slate?
You may choose whichever you desire.

    Mephistopheles: How can you so exaggerate
With such a hectic rhetoric?   500
Any little snippet is quite good—
And you sign it with one little drop of blood.

---

[18]The wager between Faust and Mephistopheles recalls that between God
and Mephistopheles in the Prologue.

Faust: If that is enough and is some use,
One may as well pander to your fad.

    Mephistopheles: Blood is a very special juice.

    Faust: Only do not fear that I shall break this
    contract.
What I promise is nothing more
Than what all my powers are striving for.
I have puffed myself up too much, it is only
Your sort that really fits my case.   510
The great Earth Spirit has despised me
And Nature shuts the door in my face.
The thread of thought is snapped asunder,
I have long loathed knowledge in all its fashions.
In the depths of sensuality
Let us now quench our glowing passions!
And at once make ready every wonder
Of unpenetrated sorcery!
Let us cast ourselves into the torrent of time,
Into the whirl of eventfulness,   520
Where disappointment and success,
Pleasure and pain may chop and change
As chop and change they will and can;
It is restless action makes the man.

    Mephistopheles: No limit is fixed for you, no bound;
If you'd like to nibble at everything
Or to seize upon something flying round—
Well, may you have a run for your money!
But seize your chance and don't be funny!

    Faust: I've told you, it is no question of happiness.   530
The most painful joy, enamored hate, enlivening
Disgust—I devote myself to all excess.
My breast, now cured of its appetite for knowledge,
From now is open to all and every smart,
And what is allotted to the whole of mankind
That will I sample in my inmost heart,
Grasping the highest and lowest with my spirit,
Piling men's weal and woe upon my neck,
To extend myself to embrace all human selves
And to founder in the end, like them, a wreck.   540

    Mephistopheles: O believe *me,* who have been
    chewing
These iron rations many a thousand year,
No human being can digest
This stuff, from the cradle to the bier.
This universe—believe a devil—
Was made for no one but a god!
He exists in eternal light
But *us* he has brought into the darkness
While *your* sole portion is day and night.

    Faust: I will all the same!   550

    Mephistopheles: That's very nice.
There's only one thing I find wrong;
Time is short, art is long.[19]
You could do with a little artistic advice.
Confederate with one of the poets
And let him flog his imagination
To heap all virtues on your head,

A head with such a reputation:
Lion's bravery,
Stag's velocity,   560
Fire of Italy,
Northern tenacity.
Let *him* find out the secret art
Of combining craft with a noble heart
And of being in love like a young man,
Hotly, but working to a plan.
Such a person—*I'd* like to meet him;
'Mr. Microcosm' is how I'd greet him.

    Faust: What am I then if fate must bar
My efforts to reach that crown of humanity   570
After which all my senses strive?

    Mephistopheles: You are in the end . . . what
    you are.
You can put on full-bottomed wigs with a million locks,
You can put on stilts instead of your socks,
You remain for ever what you are.

    Faust: I feel my endeavours have not been worth
    a pin
When I raked together the treasures of the human mind,
If at the end I but sit down to find
No new force welling up within.
I have not a hair's breadth more of height,   580
I am no nearer the Infinite.

    Mephistopheles: My very good sir, you look at
    things
Just in the way that people do;
We must be cleverer than that
Or the joys of life will escape from you.
Hell! You have surely hands and feet,
Also a head and you-know-what;
The pleasures I gather on the wing,
Are they less mine? Of course they're not!
Suppose I can afford six stallions,   590
I can add that horse-power to my score
And dash along and be a proper man
As if my legs were twenty-four.
So good-bye to thinking! On your toes!
The world's before us. Quick! Here goes!
I tell you, a chap who's intellectual
Is like a beast on a blasted heath
Driven in circles by a demon
While a fine green meadow lies round beneath.

    Faust: How do we start?   600

    Mephistopheles: We just say go—and skip.
But please get ready for this pleasure trip.

(Exit Faust)

    Only look down on knowledge and reason,
The highest gifts that men can prize,
Only allow the spirit of lies
To confirm you in magic and illusion,
And then I have you body and soul.

---

[19]An adaptation of the famous Latin aphorism "*Ars longa, vita brevis*"
("Art is long-lasting, but life is short").

Fate has given this man a spirit
Which is always pressing onwards, beyond control,
And whose mad striving overleaps   610
All joys of the earth between pole and pole.
Him shall I drag through the wilds of life
And through the flats of meaninglessness,
I shall make him flounder and gape and stick
And to tease his insatiableness
Hang meat and drink in the air before his watering lips;
In vain he will pray to slake his inner thirst,
And even had he not sold himself to the devil
He would be equally accursed.

(Re-enter Faust)

Faust: And now, where are we going?   620
Mephistopheles: Wherever you please.
The small world, then the great for us.
With what pleasure and what profit
You will roister through the syllabus!
Faust: But I, with this long beard of mine,
I lack the easy social touch,
I know the experiment is doomed;
Out in the world I never could fit in much.
I feel so small in company
I'll be embarrassed constantly.   630
Mephistopheles: My friend, it will solve itself, any
  such misgiving;
Just trust yourself and you'll learn the art of living.
Faust: Well, then, how do we leave home?
Where are your grooms? Your coach and horses?
Mephistopheles: We merely spread this mantle
  wide,
It will bear us off on airy courses.
But do not on this noble voyage
Cumber yourself with heavy baggage.
A little inflammable gas which I'll prepare
Will lift us quickly into the air.   640
If we travel light we shall cleave the sky like a knife.
Congratulations on your new course of life!

. . . .

———————◆———————

Romantic Love and Romantic Stereotypes

Romantic love, the sentimental and all-consuming passion for spiritual as well as sexual union with the opposite sex, was a favorite theme of nineteenth-century writers, painters, and composer. These artists perceived friendship, religious love, and sexual love as closely related expressions of an ecstatic harmony of souls. "In true complete love," wrote the French novelist Amantine Aurore Lucile Dupin, who used the pen name George Sand (d. 1876), "heart, mind and body meet in understanding and embrace." Love, and especially unrequited or unfulfilled love, was the subject of numerous romantic works. To name but three: Goethe's *Sorrows of Young Werther* told the story of a lovesick hero whose passion for a married woman leads him to commit suicide—the book was so popular that it made suicide something of a nineteenth-century vogue. Hector Berlioz's *Symphonie fantastique* described the composer's obsessive infatuation with a flamboyant actress (chapter 29); and Richard Wagner's opera *Tristan and Isolde* dramatized the tragic fate of two legendary medieval lovers.

Romantic writers inherited the dual view of womankind that had prevailed since the Middle Ages (chapter 11): like Eve, woman was the *femme fatale,* the seducer and destroyer of mankind; like Mary, however, woman was the source of salvation and the symbol of all that was pure and true. The Eve stereotype is readily apparent in such works as Prosper Mérimée's novel *Carmen* (on which the opera by Georges Bizet [d. 1875] was based), while the Mary stereotype is present in countless nineteenth-century stories, including *Faust* itself, where Gretchen becomes the Eternal Female, the source of procreation and personal salvation. The following lines by the German poet Heinrich Heine (d. 1856), which were set to music by his contemporary Robert Schumann (d. 1856), typify the female as angelic, ethereal, and pure—an object that thrilled and inspired the imaginations of many European romantics.

READING 103 Heine's "You are Just Like a Flower"

You are just like a flower
So fair and chaste and dear;
Looking at you, sweet sadness
Invades my heart with fear.

I feel I should be folding
My hands upon your hair,
Praying that God may keep you
So dear and chaste and fair.

———————◆———————

The nineteenth century was the first great age of women writers. Examples include the English novelists George Eliot, a pseudonym for Mary Ann Evans (d. 1880); Emily Brontë (d. 1848), author of the hypnotic novel *Wuthering Heights*; Mary Godwin Shelley (d. 1851), whose novel *Frankenstein* was mentioned earlier; and the French novelist Germaine Necker, known as Madame de Staël (d. 1817). These women often struck a startling note of personal freedom in their lives. In their novels, however, they generally tended to perpetuate the romantic stereotype of the chaste and clinging female.

George Sand addressed the popular stereotypes of womanhood from a unique perspective. She readily avowed that "Love's ideal is most certainly everlasting fidelity," and most of her more than eighty novels feature themes of romantic love and deep, undying friendship. But for some of her novels, she created heroines who freely exercised the right to love outside of marriage. These heroines did not, however, physically consummate their love, even when that love was reciprocal. Sand's heroines were very unlike Sand herself, whose numerous love affairs with leading romantic figures—including the novelist Prosper Mérimée and the composer Frederic Chopin—impassioned her life and work. Sand defied society not only by adopting a life of bohemianism and free love but also by her notorious habit of wearing men's clothes and smoking cigars (figure 28.4). The female counterpart of the Byronic hero, Sand confessed, "My emotions have always been stronger than the arguments of reason, and the restrictions I tried to impose on myself were to no avail."

Sand may have been expressing her own ambiguities concerning matters of love in her third novel, *Lélia* (1833), the pages of which are filled with the ruminations of a disenchanted heroine on the meaning of "true love." At one point in her spiritual odyssey, Lélia openly ventures:

- As I continue to live, I cannot help realizing that youthful ideas about the exclusive passion of love and its eternal rights are false, even fatal. All theories ought to be allowed. I would give that of conjugal fidelity to exceptional souls. The majority have other needs, other strengths. To those others I would grant reciprocal freedom, tolerance, and renunciation of all jealous egotism. To others I would concede mystical ardors, fires brooded over in silence, a long and voluptuous reserve. Finally, to others I would admit the calm of angels, fraternal chastity, and an eternal virginity. —Are all souls

FIGURE 28.4 *Portrait of George Sand,* Eugène Delacroix, 1830. Musée Carnavalet, Paris. Musées de la Ville de Paris © by Spadem 1991.

alike? Do all men have the same abilities? Are not some born for the austerity of religious faith, other for voluptuousness, others for work and passionate struggle, and others, finally, for the vague reveries of the imagination? Nothing is more arbitrary than the understanding of *true love*. All loves are true, whether they be fiery or peaceful, sensual or ascetic, lasting or transient, whether they lead men to suicide or pleasure. The loves *of the mind* lead to actions just as noble as the loves *of the heart*. They have as much violence and power, if not as much duration.[20]

---

[20]George Sand, *Lélia,* trans. Maria Espinosa (Bloomington, Ind.: Indiana University Press, 1978), 154–55.

Sand's works provided a wealth of information about nineteenth-century European life and culture. A prolific writer, her total output (much of which has still not been translated into English) would fill at least 150 volumes, 25 of which, each a thousand pages long, would contain her correspondence with most of the leading artists and intellectuals of her day. In addition to her novels and letters, Sand also left an autobiography and dozens of essays and articles championing socialism, women, and the working classes. She summed up the nature of romantic creativity with these words: "The writer's trade is a violent, almost indestructible passion. Once it has entered a poor head, nothing can stop it . . . long live the artist's life! Our motto is freedom."

Summary

For nineteenth-century romantics, the hero was an expression of the expansive subjectivity of the individual. Characterized by superhuman ambition and talents, the romantic hero, whether a historical figure or a fictional personality, experienced life with self-destructive intensity. Napoleon Bonaparte's remarkable career became a model for heroic action propelled by unbounded imagination and ambition. Such literary heroes as Prometheus and Faust, figures symbolizing the quest to exceed the human limits of knowledge, experience, and power, also intrigued romantic writers. The hero was a mirror image of the romantic personality, a Byronic figure with whom nineteenth-century artists identified. Byron and other romantics found in Prometheus an apt metaphor for the triumphant human spirit, while Goethe brought the legendary Faust to life as the quintessential romantic hero: a symbol of the ever-striving human will to master all forms of experience.

Romantic love was a popular theme among nineteenth-century writers, many of whom tended to stereotype females as either angels or *femmes fatales*. With George Sand, however, the romantic heroine might be a self-directed creature whose passions incited her to contemplate (if not actually exercise) sexual freedom. If, to some extent, the literature of the early nineteenth century resembles a diary that tracks the moods and passions of the romantic personality, the same is true of the other arts as well, as the next chapter will reveal.

SUGGESTIONS FOR READING

Brown, Jane K. *Goethe's Faust: The German Tragedy*. Ithaca, N.Y.: Cornell University Press, 1986.

Campbell, Joseph. *The Hero with a Thousand Faces*. 2d ed. Princeton, N.J.: Princeton University Press, 1968.

Gaull, Marilyn. *English Romanticism: The Human Context*. New York: Norton, 1988.

Newton, Eric. *The Romantic Rebellion*. New York: St. Martin's, 1963.

Pelles, Geraldine. *Art, Artists and Society: Origins of a Modern Dilemma*. Englewood Cliffs, N.J.: Prentice-Hall, Inc. 1963.

Praz, Mario. *The Romantic Agony*. Translated by Angus Davidson. New York: Oxford University Press, 1950.

Wilson, James D. *The Romantic Heroic Idea*. Baton Rouge: Louisiana State University, 1982.

29

ROMANTIC THEMES IN ART AND MUSIC

Romantic artists, like their literary counterparts, favored subjects that allowed them to explore their personal feelings and give free rein to the imagination. Nature and the natural landscape, the hero and heroism, and nationalist struggles for political independence—the very themes that captured the imagination of romantic writers—also inspired much of the art and music of the nineteenth century.

The Romantic Style in Art

Romantic artists abandoned the cool serenity of the neoclassical style in favor of emotion and spontaneity. Where neoclassicists sought symmetry and order, romantics favored irregularity and even irrationality. While neoclassical painters defined form by means of line (an artificial or "intellectual" boundary between the object and the space it occupied), romantics preferred to model form by way of color. While neoclassicists generally used shades of a single color for each individual object (coloring the red object red, for example), romantics might use touches of complementary colors to heighten the intensity of the painted object. And while neoclassical painters smoothed out brushstrokes to leave an even and polished surface finish, romantics often left their brushstrokes visible, as if to underline the spontaneity of the creative act.

Romantic artists often blurred details and exaggerated the sensuous aspects of texture and tone. Rejecting neoclassical propriety and decorum, they produced a style that made room for temperament, accident, and individual genius.

The Romantic Landscape

As a genre, landscape painting was born in eighth-century China (see chapter 14). Chinese landscapes were not literal imitations of reality but expressions of natural harmony. In the history of Chinese art, landscape painting remained for centuries an independent subject (figures 14.12, 14.13, and 14.14). By contrast, in the early history of Western art, landscape rarely enjoyed such an exalted status; rather, it usually provided the setting for important events and human actions. Not until the Renaissance—among such painters as Leonardo da Vinci, Dürer, and Brueghel—did the natural landscape become a subject in and of itself (figure 18.3). During the seventeenth century, the French academicians Poussin and Lorrain devised the ideal landscape, a genre in which nature became the theater for mythological and biblical subjects (figure 23.15). In such paintings, conception preceded design, and key elements, such as a large fore-

FIGURE 29.1 *The Haywain,* **John Constable, 1821. Oil on canvas, 51 1/2 in. × 73 in. The National Gallery, London.**

ground tree, a distant sunset, and a meandering road or stream, were arranged according to a strict set of pictorial conventions. The seventeenth-century Dutch masters Vermeer and Rembrandt rejected the ideal landscape; they painted empirically precise views of nature that advanced landscape painting as an independent genre (figure 22.9). But it was not until the nineteenth century that landscape painting became the vehicle of the artist's deepest emotions. Romantic painters translated their native affection for the countryside into scenes that ranged from the picturesque to the sublime. Like Wordsworth and Shelley, nineteenth-century painters discovered in nature a source of inspiration and a mirror of their own changing moods.

British Landscape Painting: Constable and Turner

Of the many landscape painters of the romantic era, two British figures stand out: John Constable (d. 1837) and Joseph Mallord William Turner (d. 1851). Constable owed much to the Dutch masters; yet his approach to nature was uncluttered by tradition. "When I sit down to make a sketch from nature," he wrote, "the first thing I try to do is to forget that I have ever seen a picture." Constable's freshly perceived landscapes celebrate the physical beauty of the rivers, trees, and cottages of his native Suffolk countryside even as they describe the mundane labors of its inhabitants (figure 29.1). Like Wordsworth, who tried to illustrate "incidents and situations from common life," Constable chose to paint ordinary and humble subjects—"water escaping from mill-dams, willows, old rotten planks, slimy posts, and brickwork"—as he described them. And like Wordsworth, Constable drew

FIGURE 29.2 *Wivenhoe Park, Essex,* **John Constable, 1816. Oil on canvas, 22 1/8 in. × 39 7/8 in. National Gallery of Art, Washington, D.C., Widener Collection.**

on his childhood experiences as sources of inspiration. "Painting," Constable explained, "is with me but another word for feeling and I associate 'my careless boyhood' with all that lies on the banks of the Stour [River]; those scenes made me a painter, and I am grateful."

Constable brought to his landscapes a sensitive blend of empirical detail and freedom of form. Fascinated by nineteenth-century treatises on the scientific classifications of clouds, he made numerous oil studies of cloud formations, noting on the reverse of each sketch the time of the year, hour of the day, and direction of the wind. He confessed to an "over-anxiety" about his skies and feared that he might destroy "that easy appearance which nature always has in all her movements." In order to capture the "easy appearance" of nature and the fugitive effects of light and atmosphere, Constable often stippled parts of the landscape with white dots (compare Vermeer, figure 22.9)—a device critics called "Constable's snow." His finished landscapes thus portray not so much the "look" of nature as its fleeting moods. In *Wivenhoe Park, Essex,* Constable depicts cattle grazing on English lawns that typically resemble well-manicured gardens (figure 29.2). From the distant horizon, the

residence of the owners overlooks the estate. Brilliant sunshine floods through the trees and across the fields onto a lake that is shared by swans and fishermen. But the real subject of the painting is the sky, which, with its windblown clouds, preserves the spontaneity of Constable's oil sketches.

If Constable's landscapes described nature in its humble and contemplative guises, Turner's rendered nature at its most sublime. Turner began his career making topographical drawings of picturesque and architectural subjects; these he sold to engravers, who, in turn, mass-produced and marketed them in great numbers. One of these early drawings, the ruined monastery of Tintern Abbey, calls attention to the transience of worldly beauty and reflects the romantic artist's nostalgia for the Gothic past (figure 27.1). Between 1814 and 1830, Turner traveled extensively throughout England and the Continent, making landscape studies of the mountains and lakes of Switzerland, the breathtaking reaches of the Alps, and the picturesque cities of Italy. His systematic tours inspired hundreds of rapid pencil sketches and luminous, intimate studies executed in the spontaneous (and portable) medium of watercolor.

FIGURE 29.3 *Keelmen Heaving Coals by Moonlight,* **J. M. W. Turner, 1835. Oil on canvas, 36 1/4 in. × 48 1/4 in. National Gallery of Art, Washington, D.C., Widener Collection.**

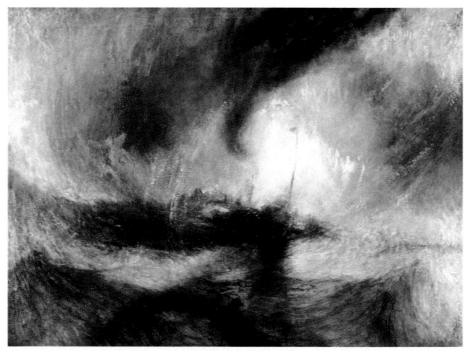

FIGURE 29.4 *Snowstorm: Steamboat off a Harbor's Mouth,* **J. M. W. Turner, 1842. Oil on canvas, 3 ft. × 4 ft. Tate Gallery, London. Art Resource, New York.**

While Turner's early works reveal a peaceful blend of poetic fantasy and fine detail (figure 29.3), his mature style investigated nature's more turbulent moods. As subjects for large-sized canvases, Turner frequently seized on natural disasters—great storms and Alpine avalanches—and human catastrophes such as shipwrecks and destructive fires. Many of his seascapes, including *Snowstorm* (figure 29.4), treat the sea as a symbol for nature's indomitable power—a favorite romantic theme, and one that prevails in Samuel Taylor Coleridge's *Rime of the Ancient Mariner* (1798), Théodore Géricault's painting, *The Raft of the*

FIGURE 29.5 *Two Men Looking at the Moon*, Caspar David Friedrich, 1819–20. Oil on panel, 11 3/4 in. × 17 1/4 in. Staatliche Kunstsammlungen, Dresden.

Medusa (figure 29.13), and Herman Melville's monumental sea novel, *Moby Dick* (1851), to name only three examples. Turner's *Snowstorm* of 1842 illustrates the extent to which the romantic artist might become intimately engaged with nature: at the age of sixty-seven Turner had himself lashed to the mast of a ship caught in a storm at sea for four hours. Turner subtitled the painting "Steam-boat off a harbor's mouth making signals in shallow water . . . the author was in this storm on the night the Ariel left Harwich." As with many of Turner's late works, *Snowstorm* was an exercise in sensation and intuition. It was the imaginative transformation of an intense physical experience, which, recollected thereafter, evoked—as Wordsworth declared—"a sense sublime/Of something far more deeply interfused,/Whose dwelling place is the light of setting suns,/And the round ocean and the living air,/And the blue sky, and in the mind of man." Indeed, Turner's "landscapes of the sublime" come closer to capturing the spirit of Wordsworth's nature mysticism than did Constable's. Their expanding and contracting forms, their swirling masses of paint, and their startling bursts of color are also comparable to the impassioned rhythms and brilliant dynamics of much romantic music.

Turner's late paintings were daringly innovative. His luminous landscapes, haunted by suggestive, "empty" spaces, had more in common with Chinese landscapes than with traditional Western ones. Critics disparagingly called Turner's transparent veils of color—vestiges of his beloved watercolors—"tinted steam" and "soapsuds." Nevertheless, in dozens of canvases that he never dared to exhibit during his lifetime, Turner all but abandoned recognizable subject matter; these experiments in light and color anticipated (and even outreached) the French impressionists by more than three decades.

Landscape Painting in Germany and France

Outside of England, German landscape artists took a more nostalgic view of nature. The paintings of Constable's contemporary, Caspar David Friedrich (d. 1840), which often include Gothic ruins and wintery graveyards, are elegiac remnants of a vanished world. In *Two Men Looking at the Moon* Friedrich boldly silhouettes two brooding figures and an ominous, half-uprooted tree against a glowing sky (figure 29.5). Somber colors add to the mood of poetic loneliness in a universe whose vast mysteries might be contemplated but never fully comprehended.

In contrast to Friedrich, French landscape painters offered a benign and gentle view of nature. The artists of the Barbizon school—named for the picturesque village on the edge of the Forest of Fontainebleau near Paris—were the first to take their easels out-of-doors.

FIGURE 29.6 *The Forest of Coubron,* Jean-Baptiste-Camille Corot, 1872. Oil on canvas, 37 3/4 in. × 30 in. National Gallery of Art, Washington, D.C., Widener Collection.

Painting directly from nature (though usually finishing the canvas in the studio), they evoked the realists' unembellished vision of the world; yet these romantic-realists were mainly concerned with capturing nature's moods. The greatest French landscape painter of the mid-nineteenth century, Jean-Baptiste-Camille Corot (d. 1875), shared the Barbizon preference for working outdoors. Corot's early landscapes, executed for the most part in Italy, were as formally composed as the paintings of Poussin and David, but they are at once simpler, more personal, and more serene. In his late canvases, Corot created landscapes that were intimate and contemplative (figure 29.6). These poetic landscapes, filled with feathery trees and misty rivers, and bathed in nuances of silver light, were so popular that Corot was able to sell as many canvases as he could paint. Even in his own time, forgeries of Corot's work abounded.

FIGURE 29.7 *The Oxbow (The Connecticut River Near Northampton),* Thomas Cole, 1836. Oil on canvas, 51 1/2 in. × 76 in. Signed and dated lower left T. Cole 1836. The Metropolitan Museum of Art, New York City, gift of Mrs. Russell Sage, 1980. (08.228)

Nineteenth-Century American Landscape Painting

American landscapes present both similarities and contrasts with those of European artists. Both reveal a clear delight in natural beauty and a fascination with nature's fleeting and dramatic moods; but American landscapes commonly reveal nature as unspoiled and resplendent. They are often more detailed and more panoramic, as if their makers felt compelled to record with photographic precision the majesty of the American continent and, at the same time, celebrate the mysteries of its untamed wilderness. Panorama and precision are features found in the topographic landscapes of the Hudson River school— a group of artists who worked chiefly in the region of upstate New York during the 1830s and 1840s. One of the leading figures of the Hudson River school was the British-born Thomas Cole (d. 1848), whose *Oxbow* offers a view of the Connecticut River near Northampton, Massachusetts (figure 29.7). In this landscape, Cole achieved a dramatic mood by framing the brightly lit hills and curving river of the distant vista with the darker motifs of an impending thunderstorm and a blighted tree.

FIGURE 29.8 *The Rocky Mountains, Lander's Peak* **Albert Bierstadt, 1863. Oil on canvas, 73 1/2 in. × 120 3/4 in. Signed and dated lower right A Bierstadt. The Metropolitan Museum of Art, Rogers Fund, 1907. 07.123**

Albert Bierstadt's landscape of the Rocky Mountains, which includes a Native American encampment in the foreground, is representative of the German-born artist's fascination with the templelike purity of America's vast, open spaces along the western frontier (figure 29.8). The isolated settlement, dwarfed and enshrined by snowcapped mountains, a magnificent waterfall, and a looking-glass lake—all bathed in golden light—is an American Garden of Eden, inhabited by tribes of unspoiled, "noble savages." The size of Bierstadt's painting (some 6 by 10 feet), signified the new importance of landscape as a genre, for, according to traditional, academic standards, large canvases were appropriate only for the representation of serious themes. Panoramic landscapes with views of exotic, faraway places were popular nineteenth-century substitutes for actual travel, and viewers were known to carry binoculars to their showings. The romantic fascination with unspoiled nature and "natural man" also inspired documentary studies of Native Americans, such as those executed by George Catlin (d. 1872) (figure 29.9). Impressed by the "silent and stoic dignity" of America's tribal peoples, Catlin went west to live among the Indians, whose lives he glorified in hundreds of drawings and paintings.

FIGURE 29.9 *The White Cloud, Head Chief of the Iowas,* **George Catlin, ca. 1845. Oil on canvas, 27 3/4 in. × 22 3/4 in. National Gallery of Art, Washington, Paul Mellon Collection.**

FIGURE 29.10 *Napoleon Visiting the Plague Victims at Jaffa,* Antoine-Jean Gros, 1804. Oil on canvas, approx. 17 ft. 5 in. × 23 ft. 7 in. Louvre. Scala/Art Resource, New York.

Heroic Themes in Art

Gros and the Glorification of the Hero

While nature and the natural landscape provided sources of artistic inspiration, so too did subjects that glorified creative individualism, patriotism, and nationalism. Napoleon Bonaparte, the foremost living hero of the age and the symbol of French nationalism, was the favorite subject of many early nineteenth-century French painters. Napoleon's imperial status was celebrated in the official portraits executed by his "first painter," Jacques-Louis David (figure 28.1); but the heroic dimension of Napoleon's career was publicized by yet another member of his staff, Antoine-Jean Gros (d. 1835). Gros' representations of Napoleon's military campaigns were the powerful vehicles of political propaganda that marked the beginning of romanticism in French painting.

Gros was a pupil of David, but, unlike David, Gros rejected the formal austerity of neoclassicism. In his monumental canvas, *Napoleon Visiting the Pesthouse at Jaffa* (1804), Gros converted a minor historical event—Napoleon's tour of his plague-ridden troops in Jaffa (in ancient Palestine)—into a major allegorical drama (figure 29.10). Casting Napoleon in the imposing guise of Christ healing the wounds of his followers, Gros framed the hero beneath the arches of an exotic Islamic arcade. He enhanced the dramatic mood of the composition by means of atmospheric contrasts of light and dark and a variety of engaging details that draw the eye deep into the background. In the foreground lie the anguished bodies of the diseased and dying, one of whom violently tears at himself. Gros' imaginative composition and painterly form anticipated the romantic style. In terms of content, Gros' *Pesthouse at Jaffa* manifested the romantic taste for themes of personal heroism, suffering, and death. When it was first exhibited in Paris, an awed public adorned the painting with palm branches and wreaths. But the inspiration for Gros' success was also the source of his undoing: after Napoleon was sent into exile, Gros' career declined, and he committed suicide by throwing himself into the River Seine.

Romantic Heroism in Goya and Géricault

Throughout most of Western history, the heroic image in art was bound up with either classical lore or Christian legend. But with Gros, we see one of the first distinctive images of heroism based on contemporary events and political conditions. The Spanish master Francisco Goya (d. 1828) helped to pioneer this phenomenon in nineteenth-century art. Having begun his career as a rococo-style tapestry designer, Goya came into prominence as court painter to the Spanish king Charles IV in Madrid. As court painter, Goya followed in the footsteps of Velásquez, despite the fact that he often brought unflattering realism to his portrait likenesses. During the latter half of his lifetime, and especially after the invasion of Spain by Napoleon's armies in 1808, Goya's art took a new turn. Horrified by the guerrilla violence of the Spanish occupation, he became a bitter social critic, producing some of the most memorable records of human warfare and savagery in the history of Western art.

The 3rd of May, 1808: The Execution of the Defenders of Madrid was Goya's response to the events following an uprising of Spanish citizens against the French army of occupation (figure 29.11). In a punitive measure, the hostile French troops rounded up Spanish suspects in the streets of Madrid, transported them to the outskirts of the city, and brutally executed them. Goya recorded the macabre episode against a dark sky and an ominous urban skyline. In the foreground, an off-center lantern forms a triangular prism of light that illuminates the fate of the Spanish rebels: some lie dead in pools of blood, while others cover their faces in fear and horror. Among the victims is the arresting figure of a young man, whose arms are flung upward in a final gesture of terror and defiance. Goya deliberately spotlights this wide-eyed and bewildered figure as he confronts imminent death. On the right, in the darkened shadows, the hulking executioners are lined up as anonymously as pieces of artillery. Goya composed the scene with an imaginative force that evoked strong feelings of sympathy and outrage. His emphatic contrasts of light and dark, his vivid use of color, and his willingness to alter details for the sake of emotional effect enhance the dramatic intensity of a contemporary event.

FIGURE 29.11 *The 3rd of May, 1808: The Execution of the Defenders of Madrid,* Francisco Goya, 1814–15. Oil on canvas, 8 ft. 9 in. × 10 ft. 4 in. Prado, Madrid.

An indictment of butchery in the name of war, *The 3rd of May, 1808* is itself restrained compared to *The Disasters of War,* a series of the etchings and **aquatints** that Goya produced in the years of the French occupation of Spain. The gruesome prints that make up *The Disasters of War* have their source in fact as well as in Goya's imagination. *Brave Deeds Against the Dead* is a shocking record of the inhumanity of Napoleon's troops, as well as a reminder that the heroes of modern warfare are often its innocent victims (figure 29.12). Rejecting David's patriotic idealism and Gros' idealized heroism, Goya launches an urgent plea for personal courage in defiance of human brutality.

Goya's contemporary, the French painter Théodore Géricault (d. 1824), further broadened the range of romantic themes. Among Géricault's favorite subjects were untamed horses and the faces of the clinically insane. Such subjects, uncommon in academic art, reflect the romantic fascination with the life that lay beyond the bounds of reason. The painting that brought Géricault instant fame, *The Raft of the Medusa,* immortalized a dramatic event that made headlines in Géricault's own time: the wreck of a government frigate called the *Medusa* and the ghastly fate of its survivors (figure 29.13). When the ship hit a reef

FIGURE 29.12 *Brave Deeds Against the Dead, Disasters of War,* Francisco Goya, ca. 1814. Etching.

fifty miles off the coast of West Africa, the inexperienced captain, a political appointee, tried to save himself and his crew, who filled the few available lifeboats. Over a hundred passengers piled onto a makeshift raft, which was to be towed by the lifeboats. Cruelly, the crew set the raft adrift. With almost no food and supplies, chances of survival were scant; after almost two weeks, in which most died and several resorted to cannibalism, fifteen survivors were rescued.

FIGURE 29.13 *The Raft of the Medusa,* Théodore Géricault, 1818–19. Oil on canvas, 16 ft. 1 in. × 23 ft. 6 in. Louvre, Paris. Giraudon/Art Resource, New York.

FIGURE 29.14 *Arabs Skirmishing in the Mountains,* Eugène Delacroix, 1863. Oil on canvas, 36 3/8 in. × 29 3/8 in. National Gallery of Art, Washington, Chester Dale Fund, 1966.

Géricault (a staunch opponent of the regime that appointed the *Medusa's* captain) was so fired by newspaper reports of the tragedy that he resolved to immortalize it. He interviewed the few survivors, made drawings of the mutilated corpses in the Paris morgue, and even had a model of the raft constructed in his studio. The result was enormous, both in size (the canvas measures 16 by 23 feet) and in dramatic impact. In the decade immediately preceding the invention of photography, Géricault provided the public with a powerful visual record of a sensational contemporary event. He organized his composition on the basis of a double triangle: one, defined by the mast and left line, incorporates the bodies of dying and the dead; the other consisted of a mass of agitated figures culminating in the magnificently painted torso of a black man who signals the distant vessel that will make the rescue. Sharp diagonals, vivid contrasts of light and dark (reminiscent of Caravaggio), and muscular nudes (inspired by Michelangelo and Rubens) heightened the emotional impact of the piece. Géricault's *Raft* elevated ordinary men to the position of heroic combatants in the eternal struggle against the forces of nature. It eulogized, moreover, the collective heroism of humble human beings confronting deadly danger, a motif equally popular in romantic literature—witness Victor Hugo's *Les Misérables* (1862).

Delacroix and the Imagery of Heroism

While Goya and Géricault democratized the image of the hero, Géricault's pupil and follower Eugène Delacroix (d. 1863) raised the hero to Byronic proportions. The most dazzling of nineteenth-century French romantic painters, Delacroix personified the romantic fascination with the sometimes terrible and violent aspects of life. A melancholic intellectual, he shared Byron's intense hatred of tyranny, his sense of alienation, his self-glorifying egotism, and his faith in the role of the imagination—features all readily discernible in the pages of his diary. In words similar to those of Byron, Wordsworth, and Goethe, Delacroix

FIGURE 29.15 *Liberty Leading the People,* Eugène Delacroix, 1830. Oil on canvas, approx. 10 ft. 8 in. × 8 ft. 6 in. Louvre, Paris.

glorified the imagination as "paramount" in the life of the artist. ". . . strange as it may seem," he observed in his diary, "the great majority of people are devoid of imagination. Not only do they lack the keen, penetrating imagination which would allow them to see objects in a vivid way—which would lead them, as it were, to the very root of things—but they are equally incapable of any clear understanding of works in which imagination predominates."[1]

Delacroix loved dramatic narrative; he favored sensuous and violent subjects drawn from contemporary life, popular literature, and ancient and medieval history. He depicted the harem women of

Islamic society, recorded the poignant and shocking results of the Turkish massacres in Greece, brought to life Dante's *Inferno,* and illustrated Goethe's *Faust* (figure 28.3). His paintings of human and animal combat, such as *Arabs Skirmishing in the Mountains,* are filled with fierce vitality and passion. Such works are faithful to his declaration, "I have no love for reasonable painting" (figure 29.14).

In his masterpiece, *Liberty Leading the People* (1830), Delacroix transformed a contemporary event, (the Revolution of 1830) into a heroic allegory of the struggle for human freedom (figure 29.15). When

[1] *The Journal of Eugène Delacroix,* trans. Lucy Norton (London: Phaidon Press, 1951), 137, 348–49.

King Louis Philippe dissolved the French legislature and took measures to repress voting rights and freedom of the press, liberal leaders, radicals, and journalists rose in rebellion. Delacroix translated this rebellion into a monumental painting that showed a handsome, bare-breasted female—the personification of Liberty—leading a group of French rebels through the narrow streets of Paris and over barricades strewn with corpses. A bayonet in one hand and the tricolor flag of France in the other, Liberty presses forward to challenge the forces of tyranny. She is champion of "the people": the middle class, as represented by the gentleman in a frock coat; the lower class, as symbolized by the scruffy youth carrying pistols; and racial minorities, as conceived in the black saber-bearer at the left. She is, moreover, France itself, the banner-bearer of the spirit of nationalism that infused nineteenth-century European history.

Delacroix's Liberty became an instant symbol of democratic aspirations. In 1884 France sent a gift of friendship to the young American nation, the monumental copper and cast-iron statue of an idealized female bearing a tablet and a flaming torch (figure 29.16). Designed by Frédéric-Auguste Bartholdi (d. 1904), *Liberty Enlightening the World* was erected on an island at the tip of Manhattan in New York City. The "sister" of Delacroix's painted heroine, the Statue of Liberty has become a classic image of freedom for homeless and oppressed people everywhere.

Like David's *Oath of the Horatii,* Delacroix's *Liberty Leading the People* delivered a heroic message. But in conception and in style, the two paintings were totally different. While David looked to the Roman past for his theme, Delacroix drew on the issues of his time, allegorizing *real* events in order to increase their dramatic impact. And whereas David's appeal was essentially elitist, Delacroix celebrated the collective heroism of ordinary people. Yet Delacroix was never a slave to the facts: although, for instance, the nudity of the fallen rebel in the left foreground (clearly related to the nudes of Géricault's *Raft*) had no basis in fact—it is uncommon to lose one's trousers in combat—the detail served to emphasize vulnerability and the imminence of death in battle. In his diary, Delacroix defended the artist's freedom to take liberties with form and content; "The most sublime effects of every master," he wrote, "are often the result of *pictorial licence;* for example, the lack of finish in Rembrandt's work, the exaggeration in Rubens. Mediocre painters never have sufficient daring, they never get beyond themselves." Stylistically, Delacroix's *Liberty* explodes with romantic passion. Surging rhythms link the smoke-filled background with the figures of the advancing rebels and the bodies of the fallen heroes heaped in the foreground. Gone are the cool restraints, the linear

FIGURE 29.16 *Statue of Liberty,* **Frédéric-Auguste Bartholdi, 1871–84. Framework constructed by A. G. Eiffel. Copper sheets mounted on steel frame, height, 152 ft. Liberty Island (Bedloe's Island), New York. National Park Service, Statue of Liberty National Monument.**

clarity, and the gridlike regularity of David's *Oath.* Gone also are the slick, finished surfaces. Delacroix's canvas resonates with dense textures and loose, rich brushstrokes. Color charges through the painting in a manner that recalls Rubens (figure 23.17), whose style Delacroix deeply admired.

The Heroic Theme in Sculpture

In sculpture as in painting, heroic subjects served the cause of nationalism. *The Departure of the Volunteers of 1792* by François Rude (d. 1855) embodied the dynamic heroism of the Napoleonic Era. Installed at the foot of the Arch of Triumph (figure 26.32), which stands at the end of the Champs Elysées in Paris, the forty-two-foot high stone sculpture commemorated the patriotism of a band of French volunteers—

FIGURE 29.17 *La Marseillaise (The Departure of the Volunteers in 1792),* François Rude, 1833–36. Stone, approx. 42 ft. × 26 ft. Arch of Triumph, Paris. Giraudon/Art Resource, New York.

presumably the battalion of Marseilles, who marched to Paris in 1792 to defend the Republic (figure 29.17). Young and old, nude and clothed in ancient and medieval garb (a device that augmented dramatic effect and universalized the heroic theme), the spirited members of this small citizen army are led by the allegorical figure of Bellona, the Roman goddess of war. Like Delacroix's Liberty, Rude's classical goddess urges the patriots onward. The vitality of the piece is enhanced by deep undercutting, which results in dramatic contrasts of light and dark. In this richly textured work, Rude captured the revolutionary spirit and emotional fervor of the marching song of this battalion, *La Marseillaise,* which the French later adopted as their national anthem.

FIGURE 29.18 Houses of Parliament, London, Charles Barry and A. W. N. Pugin, 1840–60. Length, 940 ft. © A. F. Kersting.

Trends in Nineteenth-Century Architecture

While neoclassicism dominated much of the architecture of nineteenth-century Europe and America, two other trends also prevailed. One featured a rebirth of interest in medieval, and especially Gothic, architecture. The other involved the innovative application of an exciting new structural medium: cast iron.

Nineteenth-century neomedievalism was the product of an energetic effort to revive the distinctive features of a nation's historical and cultural past. In England, where the Christian heritage of the Middle Ages was particularly strong, the search for national identity took the form of a Gothic revival in architecture. Begun in 1836, the British Houses of Parliament by Charles Barry (d. 1860) and Augustus Welby Northmore Pugin (d. 1852) were among the most aesthetically successful large-scale European public buildings in the Gothic style. The picturesque combination of spires and towers fronting on the Thames River in London was the product of Pugin's conviction that the Gothic style best expressed the dignity befitting the governmental buildings of a Christian nation (figure 29.18). The Houses of Parliament reflect the importance of historical tradition in shaping England's self-image.

FIGURE 29.19 Crystal Palace, Joseph Paxton, 1851. Photographic View of the interior. Institut für Geschichte und Theorie der Architektur an der ETH Zürich.

At the same time that most European architects were caught up in the Gothic revival, other architects were experimenting with the structural possibilities of cast iron. The new medium, which provided strength without bulk, allowed architects to span broader widths and raise structures to greater heights than those achieved by stone masonry. In England, engineers began construction on the first cast-iron suspension bridge in 1836, and by the middle of the century, iron was used for the skeletal supports of mills, warehouses, and railroad stations. Although eventually, iron would change the history of architecture more dramatically than any advance in technology since the Roman invention of concrete, Europeans were slow to realize its potential. The innovator in the use of iron for public buildings was, in

fact, not an architect but a distinguished English horticulturist and greenhouse designer named Joseph Paxton (d. 1865). Paxton's Crystal Palace, erected on-site in only nine months for the Great Exhibition of London in 1851, was the world's first prefabricated building and the forerunner of the "functional" steel and glass architecture of the twentieth century (figure 29.19). Consisting of iron ribs and 18,000 panes of glass, the 1,851-foot-long structure—its length a symbolic reference to the year of the Exhibition—resembled a gigantic greenhouse. Light entered through its transparent walls and air filtered in through louvered windows. Thousands flocked to see the Crystal Palace; yet most European architects found the glass and iron structure bizarre. Although heroic in both size and conception, the Crystal Palace had almost no impact on the architecture of its time.

FIGURE 29.20 Tower, Paris, Alexandre Gustave Eiffel, 1889. Historical Pictures Service, Inc., Chicago.

Like the Crystal Palace, the Eiffel Tower originated as a novelty. The viewing tower constructed by the engineer Gustave Eiffel (d. 1923) for the Paris World Exhibition of 1889 was, in essence, a tall (1,064 feet high), cast-iron skeleton equipped with elevators that made possible magnificent aerial views of Paris (figure 29.20). Aesthetically, the tower linked the architectural traditions of the past with those of the future: its sweeping curves, delicate tracery, and dramatic verticality recalled the glories of the Gothic cathedral, while its majestic ironwork anticipated the austere abstractions of international style architecture (chapter 32). Considered a visual monstrosity when it was first erected, the Eiffel Tower emerged as both a positive symbol of machine-age technology and as a poetic expression of the romantic imagination.

The Romantic Style in Music

"Music is the most romantic of all the arts—one might almost say, the only genuinely romantic one—for its sole subject is the infinite." Thus wrote the German novelist and musician, E. T. A. Hoffmann (d. 1822). Like many romantic composers, Hoffmann believed that music held a privileged position in its capacity to express what he called "an inexpressible longing." Music—the most abstract and elusive of the arts—was capable of freeing the intellect and speaking directly to the heart.

The nineteenth century produced an enormous amount of fine music in all genres—a phenomenon that is reflected in the fact that audiences today listen to more nineteenth-century music than to the music of any other time period. The hallmark of romantic music is personalized expression, and this feature is as apparent in large orchestral works as it is in small, intimate pieces. Like romantic poets and painters, romantic composers modified classical "rules" in order to increase expressive effects. They abandoned the precise forms and clear contours of classical music in favor of expanded or loosened forms, singable melodies, and lively rhythms. Just as romantic painters exploited color to heighten emotional impact, so composers elevated **tone color** (the distinctive quality of musical sound made by a voice, a musical instrument, or a combination of instruments) to a status equal to melody, harmony, and rhythm.

During the romantic era the orchestra grew to grand proportions. Mid-nineteenth century orchestras were often five times larger than those used by Haydn and Mozart. While the volume of sound expanded, the varieties of instrumental possibilities also grew larger, in part because of technical improvements made in the instruments themselves. The symphony and the concerto were the most important of the large compositional forms; equally popular, however, were song forms, especially songs that dealt with themes of love and death or nature and nature's moods. Romantic composers found inspiration in heroic subjects, in contemporary events, and in the legends and histories of their native lands. Like the romantic painters and writers, they favored exotic, faraway themes. Both in small musical forms and in large operatic compositions, they made every effort to achieve an ideal union of poetry and music. Finally, as if to draw attention to their own technical abilities, many romantic composers wrote music (usually for piano or violin) that only highly accomplished musicians like themselves could perform with facility.

The Music of Beethoven

The leading composer of the early nineteenth century and one of the greatest musicians of all time was the German-born Ludwig van Beethoven (d. 1827). Beethoven lived most of his life in Vienna, where he became acquainted with Mozart and studied briefly with Haydn. A skillful pianist, organist, and violinist, Beethoven composed works in almost every medium and form. His thirty-two piano sonatas tested the expressive potential of an instrument that—having acquired in the early nineteenth century an iron frame and thicker strings—was capable of extraordinary brilliance in tone.

Beethoven's greatest enterprise were his nine symphonies. These remarkable compositions generally adhered to the format of the classical symphony, but they moved beyond the boundaries of classical structure and were longer and more complex than any instrumental compositions written by Mozart and Haydn. By adding trombones and bass clarinet to the symphony orchestra and doubling the number of flutes, oboes, clarinets, and bassoons in his scoring, Beethoven vastly broadened the expressive range and dramatic power of orchestral sound. The expanded tone color and rich sonorities of Beethoven's symphonies were in part the product of such instruments as the piccolo, bass drum, and cymbals, all of which Beethoven added to the symphony orchestra.

In his use of musical **dynamics** (gradations of loudness and softness), Beethoven was more explicit and varied than his predecessors. Like most romantic writers and artists—Delacroix, in particular, comes to mind—Beethoven blurred the divisions between the structural units of a composition, exploiting textural contrasts for expressive effect. He often broke with classical form, adding, for example, a fifth movement to his Sixth (or *Pastoral*) Symphony and embellishing the finale of his Ninth Symphony with a chorus and solo voices. Beethoven's daring use of dissonances, his sudden pauses and silences, and his brilliance of thematic invention reflect his preference for dramatic spontaneity over measured regularity. The powerful opening notes of the Fifth (or C minor) Symphony—a motif that Beethoven is said to have called "fate knocking at the door"—exemplify his affection for inventive repetitions and surging rhythms that propel the music toward a powerful climax.

Like Byron and Gros, Beethoven admired Napoleon as a popular hero and a champion of liberty. In 1799, he dedicated his Symphony No. 3 in E-flat major to Napoleon, adding to the title page the subtitle, *Eroica* ("Heroic"). When Napoleon crowned himself emperor in 1804, however, Beethoven angrily scratched out the dedication, so that when the piece was published, it bore only the generalized dedication, "to the memory of a great man." Beethoven's Third Symphony is colossal in size and complexity. It follows the standard number and order of movements found in the classical symphony, but it is almost twice as long as a typical classical symphony of some twenty to twenty-five minutes. The first movement,♪ which one French critic called "the Grand Army of the soul," engages six rather than the traditional two themes dictated by the sonata form. The movement begins with two commanding hammer strikes of sound and follows with a series of themes that feature the French horn, the symbol of the hero throughout the entire piece. The second movement is a somber and solemn funeral march. For the third movement, instead of the traditional minuet, Beethoven penned a vigorous *scherzo* (in Italian, "joke"), which replaced the elegance of a courtly dance with a melody that was fast and vigorous—a joke in that it was undanceable! The last movement, a victory finale, brings the themes of the first movement together with a long coda that again features the horn. It is worth noting that for the triumphant last movement of this stirring symphony, Beethoven included musical passages originally written for a ballet on the theme of Prometheus.

Difficult as it is to imagine, Beethoven wrote much of his greatest music when he was functionally deaf. From the age of twenty-nine, when he became aware of a progressive degeneration of his hearing, he labored against depression and despair. Temperamental and defiant, Beethoven scorned the patronage system and sold his musical compositions as an independent artist. Unlike Haydn and Mozart, he declared contempt for the nobility and ignored their demands. In 1802 he confided to his family, "I am bound to be misunderstood; for me there can be no relaxation with my fellow men, no refined conversations, no mutual exchange of ideas. I must live alone like one who has been banished." In retreat from society, the alienated composer turned to nature (figure 29.21). The Weisenthal Valley of Austria was to Beethoven what the Lake District in England was to Wordsworth. In the woods outside of Vienna, Beethoven roamed with his musical sketchbook under one arm, often singing to himself in a loud voice. "Woods, trees and rock," he wrote in his diary, "give the response that man requires." Beethoven's discovery that nature mirrored his deepest emotions in-

---

♪See Music Listening Selections at end of chapter.

FIGURE 29.21 *Beethoven Composing the "Pastoral" by a Brook,* Colored lithograph from the Almanac of the Zürich Musikgesellchaft for 1834. Beethoven Haus, Bonn. H. C. Bodmer Collection.

spired his programmatic Sixth (or *Pastoral*) Symphony of 1808, which he subtitled "A recollection of country life." Each of the five movements of the *Pastoral* is labeled with a specific reference to nature: "Awakening of happy feelings on arriving in the country"; "By the brook"; "Joyous gatherings of country folk"; "Storm"; and "Shepherd's Song, happy and thankful

feelings after the storm." In the tradition of Vivaldi's *Four Seasons* (chapter 22), Beethoven imitated the sounds of nature. For example, at the end of the second movement, flute, oboe, and clarinet join to create bird calls; and a quavering *tremolo* (the rapid repetition of a tone to produce a trembling effect) on the lower strings suggests the sounds of a murmuring brook.

German Art Songs

The art songs of Beethoven's Austrian contemporary Franz Schubert (d. 1828) aptly reflect the nineteenth-century composer's desire to unite poetry and music. Schubert is credited with originating the *lied* (German for "song," pl. *lieder*), an independent song for solo voice and piano. *Lieder* were not songs in the traditional sense but, rather, poems recreated in musical terms. Their lyric qualities, like those of simple folk songs, were generated by the poem itself. The *lieder* of Schubert, Robert Schumann (d. 1856), and Johannes Brahms (d. 1897), which set to music the poetry of Heinrich Heine and Johann Goethe, among others, were intimate evocations of personal feelings and moods. Such pieces recounted tales of love and longing, described nature and its moods, or lamented the transience of human happiness.

Among Schubert's one thousand or so works (which include nine symphonies and numerous chamber pieces) are six hundred *lieder.* The song *Gretchen am Spinnrade (Gretchen at the Spinning Wheel)*⁵ is based on a poem by Goethe that occurs near the end of Part I of *Faust.* In the piece, Gretchen laments the absence of her lover Faust and anticipates the sorrows that their love will bring. Repeated three times are the poignant lines with which the song opens: "My peace is gone, My heart is sore:/I shall find it never And never more." While the melody and tone color of the voice line convey the sadness expressed in the words of the poem, the lively piano line captures the rhythms of the spinning wheel.

The Programmatic Symphonies of Berlioz

In 1830, just five years after the death of Beethoven, the French composer Hector Berlioz (d. 1869) began his first symphony. An imaginative combination of the story of Faust and Berlioz's own life, the *Symphonie fantastique* told the dramatic tale of Berlioz's "interminable and inextinguishable passion"—as he described it—for the captivating actress Henrietta Smithson. Berlioz wrote the *Symphonie* in the first flush of his passion, when he was only twenty-seven years old. Following an intense courtship, he married the woman he idolized, only to discover that he and Henrietta were dreadfully mismatched—the marriage turned Smithson into an alcoholic and Berlioz into an adulterer.

Symphonie fantastique belonged to the genre known as **program music** (instrumental music endowed with specific literary or pictorial content indicated by the composer). Berlioz was not the first to write music that was programmatic: in *The Four Seasons,* Vivaldi had linked music to poetic phrases, as had Beethoven in his *Pastoral* Symphony. But Berlioz was the first to build an entire symphony

FIGURE 29.22 *Berlioz Conducting Massed Choirs,* Gustave Doré, nineteenth-century caricature. The Bettmann Archive.

around a set of musical motifs that told a story. The popularity of program music during the nineteenth century testifies to the powerful influence of literature upon the other arts. Berlioz, whose second symphony, *Harold in Italy,* was inspired by Byron's *Childe Harold* (chapter 28), was not alone in producing such music. The Hungarian composer Franz Liszt (d. 1886) wrote symphonic poems based on the myth of Prometheus and Shakespeare's *Hamlet.* He also composed the *Faust* Symphony, which he dedicated to Berlioz. And the Russian composer Peter Ilich Tchaikovsky (d. 1893) wrote many programmatic pieces, including the tone poem *Romeo and Juliet.*

In the *Symphonie fantastique,* Berlioz linked a specific mood or event to a musical phrase, or *idée fixe* ("fixed idea"). This recurring musical motif, which Berlioz introduced within the first five minutes of the opening movement, became the means by which the composer bound together the individual parts of his dramatic narrative. Subtitled "Episode in the Life of an Artist," the *Symphonie* was an account of the young musician's opium-induced dream, in which, according to Berlioz's program notes, "the Beloved One takes the form of a melody in his mind, like a fixed idea which is ever returning and which he hears everywhere." Unified by the *idée fixe*, the *Symphonie* consists of a sequence of five parts, each distinguished by a particular mood: the lover's "reveries and passions"; a ball at which the hero meets his beloved; a stormy scene in the country; a "March to the Scaffold" (marking the hero's dream of murdering his lover and his subsequent execution);♭ and a final and feverishly orchestrated "Dream of a Witches' Sabbath" inspired by Goethe's *Faust*. (Berlioz's *Damnation of Faust*, a piece for soloists, chorus, and orchestra, likewise drew on Goethe's great drama.) The "plot" of the *Symphonie*, published along with the musical score, was featured in program notes available to listeners. But the written narrative was *not* essential to the enjoyment of the music, for as Berlioz himself explained, the music held authority as absolute sound, above and beyond its programmatic associations.

Berlioz, the spiritual heir to Beethoven, took liberties with traditional symphonic form. He composed the *Symphonie* in five movements instead of the usual four and combined instruments inventively so as to create unusual sets of sound. In the third movement of the *Symphonie*, a solo English horn and four kettledrums produce the effect of "distant thunder". He also expanded tone color, stretching the register of clarinets to screeching highs, for instance, and playing the strings of the violin with the wood of the bow instead of with the hair. Berlioz's favorite medium was the full symphony orchestra, which he enlarged to include 150 musicians. Called "the apostle of bigness," Berlioz's *ideal* orchestra consisted of over 400 musicians, including 242 string instruments, thirty pianos, thirty harps, and a chorus of 360 voices. The monumental proportions of Berlioz's orchestras drew spoofs in contemporary cartoons, such as that by the French illustrator Gustave Doré (figure 29.22). But Berlioz, who was also a talented writer and a music critic for Parisian newspapers, thumbed his nose at the critics in lively essays that defended his own musical philosophy.

The Piano Music of Chopin

If the nineteenth century was the age of romantic individualism, it was also the age of the **virtuoso**. In music, this meant that talented composers wrote music that might be performed gracefully and accurately only by individuals with extraordinary technical skills. One such individual was the Polish-born composer Frédéric Chopin (d. 1849). At the age of seven, Chopin gave his first piano concert in Warsaw.

FIGURE 29.23 *Frédéric Chopin,* Eugène Delacroix, 1838. Oil on canvas, 18 in. × 15 in. Louvre, Paris. Giraudon/Art Resource, New York.

Slight in build even as an adult, Chopin had small hands that nevertheless could reach like "the jaws of a snake" (as one of his peers observed) across the keys of the piano. After leaving Warsaw, Chopin became the acclaimed pianist of the Paris *salons* and a close friend of Delacroix (who painted his portrait—figure 29.23), Berlioz, and many of the leading novelists of his age, including George Sand (chapter 27), with whom he had a stormy nine-year love affair.

In his brief lifetime—he died of tuberculosis at the age of thirty-nine—Chopin created an entirely personal musical idiom linked to the expressive potential of the modern piano. For the piano, the favorite single instrument of the nineteenth century, Chopin wrote over two hundred pieces, most of which were small, intimate works, such as dances, **preludes** (short keyboard pieces in one movement), **nocturnes** (slow, songlike pieces), **impromptus** (short keyboard compositions that sound improvised), and **études** (instrumental studies designed to improve a player's technique). Chopin's *Étude in G-Flat Major,* **Opus** 10, Number 5♭ is a breathtaking piece that challenges the performer to play very rapidly on the black

---

♭See Music Listening Selections at end of chapter.

♭See Music Listening Selections at end of chapter.

FIGURE 29.24 **The Facade of the Paris Opéra, Charles Garnier, 1865–75. Giraudon/Art Resource, New York.**

keys, which are less than half the width of the white keys.

Just as Delacroix's paintings, though carefully contrived, give the impression of spontaneity, so Chopin's music seems improvised—the impetuous record of fleeting feeling, rather than the studied results of diligent construction. And, as in Delacroix's art, Chopin's pieces are marked by fresh turns of harmony and free tempos and rhythms. Chopin might embellish a melodic line with unusual and flamboyant devices, such as a rolling *arpeggio* (the sounding of the notes of a chord in rapid succession). His preludes feature bold contrasts of calm meditation and bravura, while his nocturnes—like the romantic landscapes of Friedrich and Corot (figures 29.5 and 29.6)—are dreamy and wistful. Of his dance forms, the polonaise and the mazurka preserve the robustness of the folk tunes of his native Poland, while the waltz mirrors the romantic taste for a new type of dance, more sensuous and expressive than the courtly and formal minuet.

Considered vulgar and lewd when it was introduced in the late eighteenth century, the waltz, with its freedom of movement and intoxicating rhythms, became the most popular of all nineteenth-century dances.

The Romantic Ballet

The theatrical art form known as "ballet" (see chapters 17 and 23) reached immense popularity in the Age of Romanticism. While the great ballets of Tchaikovsky—*Swan Lake, The Nutcracker,* and *Sleeping Beauty*—were performed in Russia at the end of the century, it was in nineteenth-century Paris that romantic ballet was born. By the year 1800, ballet had moved from the court to the theater, where it was enjoyed as a middle-class entertainment. Magnificent theaters, such as the Paris Opéra, completed in 1875 by Charles Garnier (d. 1898), became showplaces for public entertainment (figure 29.24). The neobaroque façade reflected Garnier's awareness that Greek ar-

FIGURE 29.25 Paris, the Opéra, 1862–75, Charles Garnier; the Grand Staircase in an engraving of 1880. Charles Garnier, *Le Nouvel Opéra de Paris.* Paris, 1880, Vol. 2, plate 8.

chitects had painted parts of their buildings, but the glory of the structure was its interior, which took as its focus a sumptuous grand staircase (figure 29.25). Luxuriously appointed, and illuminated by means of the latest technological invention, gaslight, the Paris Opéra became the model for public theaters throughout Europe. For the façade, Jean Baptiste Carpeaux (d. 1875) created a fifteen-foot-high sculpture whose exuberant rhythms capture the spirit of the dance as the physical expression of human joy (figure 29.26).

The ballets performed on the stage of the Paris Opéra launched a Golden Age in European dance. In Paris in 1832 the Italian-born ***prima ballerina*** (the first, or leading female dancer in a ballet company) Maria Taglioni (d. 1871) perfected the art

FIGURE 29.26 *The Dance,* Jean Baptiste Carpeaux, 1867–69. Stone, created for the facade of the Opéra, Paris. Now in Musée de l'Opéra. Giraudon/Art Resource, New York.

the angelic female—a fictional creature drawn from fable and fantasy. The sylph in *La Sylphide* was a mythical nature deity who was thought to inhabit the air, as, for instance, nymphs were thought to inhabit the woodlands. In *La Sylphide,* a sylph enchants the hero and lures him away from his bride-to-be. Pursued by the hero, she nevertheless evades his grasp and dies—the victim of a witch's malevolence—before their love is consummated. The heroine of *La Sylphide* (and other romantic ballets), along with the *prima ballerina* who assumed that role, were symbols of the elusive ideals of love and beauty sought by such romantics as Byron and Keats (chapters 27 and 28). She conformed as well to the stereotype of the pure and innocent female found in the pages of Sand's romantic novels. The traditional equation of beauty and innocence in the person of the idealized female is well illustrated in the comments of one French critic, who described "the aerial and virginal grace of Taglioni," and exulted, "She flies like a spirit in the midst of transparent clouds of white muslin—she resembles a happy angel." Clearly, the nineteenth-century ballerina was the romantic realization of the Eternal Female, a figure that fit the stereotype of the angelic woman.

FIGURE 29.27 Maria Taglioni in her London debut of 1830. Bibliotheque Nationale, Paris.

of dancing *sur les points* ("on the toes") (figure 29.27). Taglioni's performance in the ballet *La Sylphide* (choreographed by her father) was hailed as nothing less than virtuoso. Clothed in a diaphanous dress with a fitted bodice and a bell-shaped skirt—the prototype of the *tutu*—Taglioni performed perfect **arabesques**—a ballet position in which the dancer stands on one leg with the other extended in back and one or both arms are held to create the longest line possible from one extremity to the other. She also astonished audiences by crossing the stage in three magnificent, floating leaps. While faithful to the exact steps of the classical ballet, Taglioni brought to dance the new, more sensuous spirit of nineteenth-century romanticism.

Popular legends and fairy tales inspired many of the ballets of the romantic era, including *La Sylphide, Giselle,* and the more widely known *Swan Lake* and *Sleeping Beauty,* composed by Tchaikovsky. The central figure of each ballet was usually some version of

Romantic Opera

Verdi and Italian Grand Opera

Romantic opera, designed to appeal to a growing middle-class audience, came into existence after 1820. The culmination of baroque theatricality, romantic opera was "grand" both in size and in spirit. It was a flamboyant spectacle that united all aspects of theatrical production—music, dance, stage sets, and costumes. While Paris was the operatic capital of Europe in the first half of the nineteenth century, Italy ultimately took the lead in seducing the public with hundreds of wonderfully tuneful and melodramatic romantic operas.

The leading Italian composer of the romantic era was Giuseppe Verdi (d. 1901). In Verdi's twenty-six operas, including *Rigoletto* (1851), *La Traviata* (1853), and *Otello* (1887), the long, unbroken Italian operatic tradition that began with Monteverdi (chapter 20) came to its peak. Reflecting on his gift for capturing high drama in music, Verdi exclaimed, "Success is impossible for me if I cannot write as my heart dictates." The heroines of Verdi's operas, also creatures of the heart, usually die for love. Perhaps the most famous of Verdi's operas is *Aida,* which was commissioned in 1870 by the Turkish viceroy of Egypt to mark the opening of the Suez Canal. *Aida* made a nationalistic plea for unity against foreign domination—one critic called the opera "agitator's music." Indeed, the aria *"O Patria Mia"* ("O my country") is an expression of Verdi's ardent love for the newly unified Italy. But *Aida* is also the passionate love story of an Egyptian prince and an Ethiopian princess held as a captive slave. Verdi's stirring arias, vigorous choruses, and richly colored orchestral passages can be enjoyed by listening alone, but the dramatic force of this opera can only be appreciated by witnessing first-hand a theatrical performance—especially one that engages such traditional paraphernalia as horses, chariots, and, of course, elephants.

Wagner and the Birth of Music-Drama

In Germany the master of grand opera and one of the most formidable composers of the century was Richard Wagner (d. 1883). The stepson of a gifted actor, Wagner spent much of his childhood composing poems and plays and setting them to music. This union of music and literature culminated in the birth of what Wagner called **music-drama**, a unique synthesis of sound and story. Wagner drew on romantic themes from German history and legend. He wrote his own librettos and composed scores that brought to life the events and personalities featured in his stories. His aim, as he himself explained, was

FIGURE 29.28 1989 New York Metropolitan Opera production of Wagner's *Das Rheingold,* from *The Ring of the Nibelung.* © Beth Bergman, 1991.

"to force the listener, for the first time in the history of opera, to take an interest in a poetic idea, by making him follow all its developments" as dramatized simultaneously in sound and story.

Of Wagner's nine principal operas, his greatest is a monumental, fifteen-hour cycle of four music-dramas collectively titled *Der Ring des Nibelungen* (*The Ring of the Nibelung*). Based on Norse and Germanic mythology, *The Ring* involves the quest for a magical but accursed golden ring, the power of which would provide its possessor with the potential to control the universe. Out of a struggle between the gods of Valhalla and a race of giants emerges the hero, Siegfried, whose valorous deeds secure the ring for his lover Brünhilde (figure 29.28). In the end Siegfried loses both his love and his life, and Valhalla crumbles in flames, destroying the gods and eliciting the birth of a new order. Like Goethe, whose *Faust* was a lifetime effort and a tribute to his nation's past, Wagner toiled on the monumental *Ring* for over twenty-five years, from 1848 to 1874.

Awesome in imaginative scope, *The Ring* brings to life some of the hero myths that shaped the Western, and especially Germanic, literary tradition. But even more extraordinary than the theme of *The Ring* is its music, which matched its poetry in scope and drama. According to Wagner, heroic music was made possible only by a heroic orchestra—his totaled 115 pieces, including 64 strings. Unlike Verdi, whose operas generally reflected nineteenth-century musical practice, Wagner's music-dramas anticipated some of the more radical experiments of the twentieth century, including the dissolution of classical tonality (chapter 32). In fact, Wagner's music-dramas shattered traditional Western operatic techniques. Whereas composers normally divided the dramatic action into recitatives, arias, choruses, and instrumental passages, with the vocal line predominating, the mature Wagner gave the entire dramatic action to the orchestra, which engulfs the listener with a maelstrom of uninterrupted melody. In Wagner's operas, the vocal line is blended with a continuous orchestral line. Character and events emerge with clarity, however, owing to Wagner's use of *leitmotifs* (German for "leading motifs"), short musical phrases that—like Berlioz's *idées fixe*—designate a particular person, thing, or idea in the story. *The Ring*, which features a total of twenty *leitmotifs*, is a complex web of dramatic and musical themes. "Every bar of dramatic music," Wagner proclaimed, "is justified only by the fact that it explains something in the action or in the character of the actor." The artist's mission, insisted Wagner, was to communicate "the necessary spontaneous emotional mood"; and in his expressive union of poetry and music, Wagner fulfilled that mission.

Summary

The themes of nature, heroism, and nationalism dominated the arts of the romantic era. Romantic artists generally elevated the heart over the mind and the emotions over the intellect. They favored subjects that gave free rein to the imagination, to the mysteries of the spirit, and to the cult of the ego. Increasingly independent of the official sources of patronage, they regarded themselves as the heroes of their age and often turned their works into autobiographical expressions of their own thoughts, dreams, and feelings.

Romantic artists made the natural landscape an independent subject in Western art. The European landscape painters Constable, Turner, Friedrich, and Corot explored nature's moods as metaphors for human feeling. In the landscapes of the Americans Cole and Bierstadt, nature became the symbol of an unspoiled and rapidly vanishing world. Romantic artists also favored heroic themes and personalities, especially those that illustrated the struggle for political independence. Gros, Géricault, Goya, and Delacroix stretched the bounds of traditional subject matter to include controversial contemporary events, exotic subjects, and medieval legends. Delacroix's *Liberty Leading the People* and Rude's *Departure of the Volunteers of 1792* are quintessential examples of the spirit of nationalism that swept through nineteenth-century Europe. The search for national identity is also evident in the Gothic revival in architecture. The neoGothic movement paid homage to Europe's historic past, even as Paxton's Crystal Palace, the world's first prefabricated building, offered a prophetic glimpse into the future. Just as romantic artists preferred themes that elevated spontaneous emotion over poised objectivity, so too they favored freedom in composition and technique. Romantic painters, for instance, rejected neoclassical rules of balance and clarity in composition and tended to model forms by means of bold color and vigorous brushwork.

Romantic composers, like other romantic artists, found inspiration in heroic and nationalistic themes, as well as in nature's moods and the vagaries of human love. In their desire to express strong personal emotions, they often abandoned classical models and stretched musical forms to fit their feelings. The enlargement of the symphony orchestra in size and expressive range is apparent in the works of Beethoven, Berlioz, and Wagner. Berlioz's *idée fixe* and Wagner's *leitmotif* tied sound to story, evidence of the romantic search for an ideal union of poetry and music. Lyrical melodies and tone color became as important to romantic music as the free use of form and color were to romantic painters. Schubert united poetry and music in the intimate form of the *lied,* while Chopin captured a vast range of moods and emotions in expressive piano pieces, many of which required great virtuosity to perform.

Two of the most popular forms of musical expression in the nineteenth century were ballet and opera. Romantic ballet, which featured themes drawn from fantasy and legend, came to flower in France and, later, in Russia. Grand opera was brought to its peak in Italy by Verdi and in Germany by Wagner, both of whom exploited nationalistic themes. The fact that so much nineteenth-century art, music, and dance is still enjoyed today reflects the strength of romanticism both as a style and as an attitude of mind.

GLOSSARY

aquatint   a type of print produced by an engraving method similar to etching but involving finely granulated tonal areas rather than line alone

arabesque   in ballet, a position in which the dancer stands on one leg with the other extended in back and one or both arms held to create the longest line possible from one extremity of the body to the other

arpeggio   the sounding of the notes of a chord in rapid succession

dynamics   the gradations of loudness or softness with which music is performed

étude   (French, "study") an instrumental study designed to improve a player's performance technique

impromptu   (French, "improvised") a short keyboard composition that sounds as if it were improvised

lied   (German, "song," pl. "*lieder*") an independent song for solo voice and piano; also known as "art song"

leitmotif   (German, "leading motif") a short musical theme that designates a person, object, place, or idea and that reappears throughout a musical composition

music-drama   a unique synthesis of sound and story in which both are developed simultaneously and continuously; a term used to describe Wagner's later operas

nocturne   a slow, songlike piece, usually written for piano; the melody is played by the right hand, and a steady, soft accompaniment is played by the left

opus   (Latin, "work") a musical composition; followed by a number, it designates either the chronological place of a musical composition in the the composer's total musical output or the order of its publication; often abbreviated "op."

prelude   a short, independent piano composition in one movement

prima ballerina   the first, or leading female dancer in a ballet company

program music   instrumental music endowed with specific literary or pictorial content that is indicated by the composer

scherzo   (Italian, "joke") in Beethoven's music, a sprightly, lively musical melody

tone color   the distinctive quality of musical sound made by a voice, a musical instrument, or a combination of instruments; also called *timbre* (see chapter 13)

tremolo   in music, the rapid repetition of a single pitch or two pitches alternately, producing a trembling effect

virtuoso   one who exhibits great technical ability, especially in musical performance; also, a musical composition demanding (or a performance demonstrating) great technical skill

SUGGESTIONS FOR READING

Clark, Kenneth. *The Romantic Rebellion: Romantic Versus Classic Art.* New York: Harper, 1986.

Conrad, Peter. *Romantic Opera and Literary Form.* Berkeley, Calif.: University of California Press, 1977.

Einstein, Alfred. *Music in the Romantic Era.* New York: Norton, 1947.

Friedlander, Walter. *David to Delacroix.* Translated by Robert Goldwater. Cambridge, Mass.: Harvard University Press, 1952.

Kerman, Joseph, and Alan Tyson. *The New Grove Beethoven.* London: Macmillan, 1983.

Longyear, Rey. *Nineteenth-Century Romanticism in Music.* Englewood Cliffs, N.J.: Prentice-Hall, 1973.

Migel, Parmenia. *The Ballerinas: From the Court of Louis XIV to Pavlova.* New York: Macmillan, 1972.

Novak, Barbara. *American Painting of the Nineteenth Century: Realism, Idealism, and the American Experience.* New York: Praeger, 1969.

Plantinga, Leon. *Romantic Music.* New York: Norton, 1982.

Rosenthal, Michael. *Constable: the Painter and his Landscape.* New Haven, Conn.: Yale University Press, 1983.

Shanes, Eric. *Turner's Human Landscape.* London: Heinemann, 1990.

Vaughan, William. *Romantic Art.* London: Thames and Hudson, 1978.

Weber, William. *Music and the Middle Classes: The Social Structure of Concert Life in London, Paris and Vienna.* New York: Holmes Meier, 1975.

MUSIC LISTENING SELECTIONS

Cassette II Selection 11. Beethoven, Symphony No. 3, in E-flat Major, *Eroica,* 1st Movement, Allegro (1803–04).

Cassette II Selection 12. Schubert, *Gretchen am Spinnrade* (1814).

Cassette II Selection 13. Berlioz, *Symphonie fantastique,* Op. 14, "March to the Scaffold," 4th Movement (1830).

Cassette II Selection 14. Chopin, *Étude in G-flat Major,* Op. 10, No. 5 (1833).

30

VARIETIES OF REALISM

While the romantic movement dominated the nineteenth century, still another point of view, that of *realism*, challenged the prevailing emphasis on subjectivity, exoticism, and escapism. *Realists* called for fidelity to nature and an unidealized assessment of contemporary life. They insisted on a clear-eyed attention to social problems, especially those related to the combined effects of nineteenth-century European nationalism and the Industrial Revolution.

Nations had long drawn their strength and identity from their economic and military superiority over other nations. In the decades following the American and French revolutions, nationalism and the quest for national identity spurred movements for popular sovereignty. But a more aggressive form of nationalism marked the late nineteenth century. Fueled by advancing industrialism, nations not only continued to compete among themselves for economic and political preeminence, but they also sought control of markets throughout the world. The combined effects of nationalism, industrialism, and the consequent phenomenon of European colonialism influenced the direction of modern Western history and that of the world beyond the West as well.

The Global Dominion of the West

Advancing Industrialism

Industrialism provided the economic and military basis for the West's rise to a position of dominance over the rest of the world. This process is well illustrated in the history of the railroad, the most important technological phenomenon of the early nineteenth century and one made possible by the combined technologies of steam power, coal, and iron. The first all-iron rails were cast in England in 1767, but it was not until 1804 that the English built their first steam railway locomotive, and several more decades until "iron horses" became a major mode of transportation. By 1830, thousands of miles of railroad track linked England's major cities. The drive to build national railways spread throughout much of Europe and North America. By 1850, twenty-three thousand miles of railway track crisscrossed Europe, linking the sources of raw materials to factories and markets. In the coal mining region of the Ruhr Valley in Northern Germany and across the vast continent of North America, railroads facilitated economic and political expansion. As Western nations colonized other parts of the globe, they brought with them the railroad and other agents of industrialism.

FIGURE 30.1 Guaranty Building, Buffalo, New York, Louis Henry Sullivan and Dankmar Adler, 1894–95. Collection, David R. Phillips, Chicago Architectural Photographing Company.

If the railroad was the prime symbol of advancing industrialism, the skyscraper became the unique emblem of modern corporate power. Skyscrapers were made possible by the technology of steel, a medium that was perfected in 1856. Lighter, stronger, and more resilient than cast iron, steel could carry the entire weight of a structure, thus eliminating the need for solid, weight-bearing walls. Steel made possible a whole new concept of building design characterized by lighter materials, flat roofs, and large windows. In the 1880s, architects and engineers in Chicago combined the new steel frame with the electric elevator (invented in 1852) to produce the skyscraper. In 1885, William Le Baron Jenney (d. 1907) built the first definitive steel-frame skyscraper, the Home Insurance Building in Chicago, which, ironically, hid its metal skeleton beneath a traditional looking brick and masonry facade. His follower, Louis Henry Sullivan (d. 1924) created a series of distinctive multi-story buildings whose exteriors proudly reflected the structural simplicity of their steel frames (figure 30.1). Within decades, the American skyscraper became the hallmark of modern urban culture.

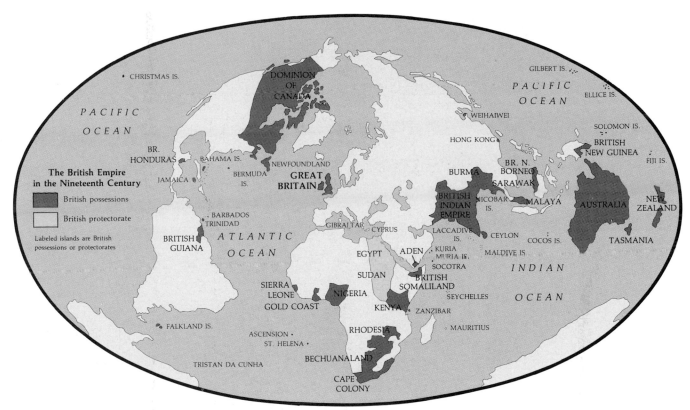

MAP 30.1 The British Empire, nineteenth century.

By 1880, Western technology included the internal combustion engine, the telegraph, the telephone, the camera, and, perhaps most significant for the everyday life of human beings: electricity. Processed steel, aluminum, the steam turbine, and the pneumatic tire—all products of the 1880s—further altered the texture of life in the industrialized world. These devices, along with more lethal instruments of war such as the fully automatic "machine gun," gave Europe clear advantage over other parts of the globe and facilitated Western imperialism in less industrially developed areas. In the enterprise of imperialism, the industrialized nations of Great Britain, France, Belgium, Germany, Italy, and the United States took the lead.

Colonialism

The history of European expansion into Asia, Africa, and other parts of the globe dates back at least to the Age of the Renaissance. Between approximately 1500 and 1800, Europeans established trading outposts in Africa, China, and India. But not until after 1800, in the wake of the Industrial Revolution, did European imperialism transform the territories of foreign powers into outright colonial possessions. The need for raw materials and markets for manufactured goods prompted the industrialized nations to colonize vast

parts of Asia, Africa, and other localities. So massive was this effort that by the end of the nineteenth century, the West had established economic, political, and cultural dominance over much of the civilized world.

European imperialists defended the economic exploitation of weaker countries with the view, inspired by social Darwinism, that in politics, as in nature, the strongest or "most fit" emerged in the "struggle for survival." Since those of the Caucasian race had proven themselves the "most fit," they argued, it was the white person's "burden" to rule over the "less fit" nonwhite peoples of the earth. Britain, the leader in European industrialization, spearheaded the thrust toward colonization. The first major civilization to be subjugated by Britain was India, and by 1870, British imperialists had established control over so much territory across the globe that they claimed "the sun never set" on the British Empire (Map 30.1). While British policy in India moved from commerce to conquest and rule, France, Belgium, and Germany seized most of Africa; and the European powers, along with Russia and Japan, carved out trade concessions in China. In 1853, the United States (itself a colony of Britain until 1776), forced Japan to open its doors to Western trade; and, at the end of the century, America established its own overseas empire in the Philippines and Cuba.

FIGURE 30.2 *Iron Mill*, Adolph Friedrich Erdmann von Menzel (*Das Eisenwerk*), 1875. Oil on canvas, 60 1/4 in. × 99 5/8 in. National Gallery, Berlin.

Although Westerners rationalized their imperialistic policies by contending that they were "civilizing" the backward peoples of the globe, in fact, they usually contributed to undermining cultural traditions and to humiliating and often enfeebling the civilizations they dominated. In China, for instance, the Europeans introduced cheap textiles and opium and enforced trade policies that delayed any Chinese initiative toward industrialization. In Africa, European powers established economic authority, as well as control over labor, often redrawing territorial boundaries with little regard for native populations. Foreign companies leased large tracts of lands from which native goods such as rubber, diamonds, and gold might be extracted; and increasingly Africans were forced to work on white-owned plantations and mines. To the European mind, the benefits of Western science, technology, and religion far outweighed the negative impact of colonialism. But the "gift" of progress proved destructive to its recipients. Few significant developments took place in the arts of India, China, and Africa during the nineteenth century; indeed, in general, there was a marked decline in productivity and originality. The full consequences of Western colonialism in Africa and Asia, however, would not become clear until the twentieth century (chapter 34).

Social and Economic Realities

In global terms, advancing industrialization polarized the nations of the world into the technologically advanced—the "haves"—and the technologically backward—the "have-nots." But industrialization had an equally profound impact within the industrialized nations themselves: it changed the nature and character of human work, altered relationships between human beings, and affected the natural environment. Prior to 1800 the practice of accumulating capital for industrial production and commercial profit played only a limited role in European societies. But after 1800, industrial production, enhanced by advances in machine technology, came to be controlled by a relatively small group of middle-class **entrepreneurs** (those who organize, manage, and assume the risks of a business) and by an even smaller number of **capitalists** (those who provide investment capital). In-

FIGURE 30.3 *The Weavers Cycle: March of the Weavers,* Käthe Kollwitz, 1897. Etching, 8 3/4 in. × 11 5/8 in. The University of Michigan Museum of Art, Ann Arbor. 1956/1.21.

dustrialization created wealth, but that wealth was concentrated in the hands of a small minority of the population. The vast majority of men and women lived hard lives supported by meager wages—the only thing they had to sell was their labor. Factory laborers, including women and children, worked under dirty and dangerous conditions for long hours—sometimes up to sixteen per day (figure 30.2). Mass production brought more (and cheaper) goods to more people more rapidly, ultimately raising the standard of living in industrialized nations. But European industrialism and the unequal distribution of wealth contributed to a dramatic gap between capitalist entrepreneurs—the "haves" of society—and the working classes—the "have-nots." In 1846, the British statesman Benjamin Disraeli (d. 1881) described England under the rule of Queen Victoria (d. 1901) as two nations: the nation of the poor and the nation of the rich.

Beginning in 1848, the lower classes protested against these conditions with sporadic urban revolts. Economic unrest prevailed not only in the cities but in rural areas as well, where agricultural laborers were often treated like slaves—in the United States, until the Emancipation Proclamation of 1863, they *were* in fact slaves. Between 1855 and 1861, there were almost five hundred peasant uprisings across Europe (figure 30.3). Reform, however, was slow in coming. Outside of England, in Germany, for instance, trade unions and social legislation to benefit the working class did not appear until 1880 or later, while in Russia, economic reform would require nothing less than a full-scale revolution.

Nineteenth-Century Social Theory

Among nineteenth-century European intellectuals there developed a serious debate over how to address the social results of industrial capitalism. Matters of social reform were central to the development of nineteenth-century ideologies, or doctrines, that dictated specific policies of political and economic action. Traditional *conservatives* stressed the importance of maintaining order and perpetuating conventional power structures and religious authority. *Liberals,* on the other hand, whose ideas were rooted in Englightenment theories of human progress and perfectibility (see chapter 24), supported gradual reform through enlightened legal systems, constitutional guarantees, and a generally equitable distribution of material benefits. The British liberal Jeremy Bentham (d. 1832) advanced the doctrine of *utilitarianism,* which held that governments should work to secure "the greatest happiness for the greatest number of people"; while Bentham's student, John Stuart Mill (d. 1873), expounded the ideology of social liberalism. Mill emphasized freedom of thought over equality and personal happiness. He held that individuals must be free to direct their own lives, but, recognizing the disadvantages that might result from free competition, he argued that the state must protect its weaker members by acting to regulate the economy where private initiative failed to do so. Mill feared that the general will—the will of unenlightened, propertyless masses—might itself prove tyrannous and oppressive. He concluded, therefore, in his classic statement of the liberal creed, *On Liberty* (1859), that "as soon as any part of a person's conduct affects prejudicially the interests of others, society has jurisdiction over it." For Mill, as for most nineteenth-century liberals, governments must intervene to safeguard and protect the wider interests of society.

Such theories met with strenuous opposition from the *socialists.* For the latter, neither conservatism nor liberalism responded adequately to current social and economic inequities. Socialists attacked capitalism as unjust; they called for the common ownership and administration of the means of production and distribution in the interest of the public good. Society, according to the socialists, should operate entirely in the interest of the needs of the people, communally and cooperatively, rather than competitively. Such utopian socialists as Pierre Joseph Proudhon (d. 1865) envisioned a society free of state control, while the more extreme *anarchists* favored the complete dissolution of the state and the elimination of the force of law.

The Radical Views of Marx and Engels

The German theorist Karl Marx (d. 1883) agreed with the socialists that bourgeois capitalism corrupted humanity, but his theory of social reform was an even more radical version of socialism, for it involved a violent revolution that would both destroy the old order and usher in a new society. Marx began his career by taking a degree in philosophy at the University of Berlin. Moving to Paris, he became a lifelong friend of the social scientist and journalist Friedrich Engels (d. 1895). Marx and Engels shared a similar critical attitude toward the effects of European industrial capitalism. By 1848, they completed *The Communist Manifesto,* a short treatise published as the platform of a workers' association called the Communist League. *The Manifesto,* which still remains the "guidebook" of Marxian socialism, demanded the "forcible overthrow of all existing social conditions" and the liberation of the **proletariat**, or working class. Marx offered an even more detailed criticism of the free enterprise system in *Das Kapital,* a work on which he toiled for thirty years.

Marx's writings had enormous practical and theoretical influence. They not only supplied a justification for lower-class revolt, but they brought attention to the role of economics in the larger life of a society. Marx described human behavior and human history in exclusively materialistic terms, arguing that the conditions under which one earned a living determined all other aspects of life: social, political, and cultural. A student of the Hegelian dialectic (chapter 27), Marx viewed history as a struggle between "haves" (thesis) and "have-nots" (antithesis) that would resolve in the synthesis of a classless society. From Hegel, Marx derived the utopian idea of the perfectibility of the state. The end product of dialectical change, argued Marx, was a society free of class antagonisms and the ultimate dissolution of the state itself.

The Communist Manifesto is a condemnation of the effects of capitalism on the individual and the society at large. The first section of the treatise (part of which is included in Reading 104) defends the claim that "the history of all hitherto existing society is the history of class struggles." The authors explain how capitalism concentrates wealth in the hands of the few, providing great luxuries for some, while creating an oppressed and impoverished proletariat. The psychological effects of such circumstances, they contend, are devastating: bourgeois capitalism alienates workers from their own productive efforts and robs individuals of their basic humanity. Finally, the authors call for violent revolution by which workers will seize the instruments of capitalistic production and abolish private ownership.

Although Marx and Engels failed to anticipate capitalism's potential to spread rather than to limit wealth, their manifesto gave sharp focus to prevailing class differences and to the actual condition of the European economy of their time. And despite the fact that Marx and Engels did not provide an explanation of exactly *how* their classless society might function, their call to revolution would be heeded in the decades to come. Oddly enough, Communist revolutions would occur in some of the least industrialized countries of the world, such as Russia and China, rather than in the most industrialized countries, as Marx and Engels anticipated. Elsewhere, Communists would operate largely by *nonrevolutionary* vehicles, such as labor unions and political organizations, to initiate better working conditions, higher wages, and greater social equality. But the anti-Communist revolutions of the late twentieth century and the recent collapse of the Communist government in the Soviet Union reveal mounting frustration with the failure of most Communist regimes to raise economic standards among the masses.

READING 104 From Marx's and Engels' *Communist Manifesto*

I. Bourgeois and Proletarians[1]

The history of all hitherto existing society is the history of class struggles.

Freeman and slave, patrician and plebeian, lord and serf, guild-master[2] and journeyman, in a word, oppressor and oppressed, stood in constant opposition to one another, carried on an uninterrupted, now hidden, now open fight, a fight that each time ended either in a revolutionary reconstitution of society at large or in the common ruin of the contending classes.

In the earlier epochs of history we find almost   10 everywhere a complicated arrangement of society into various orders, a manifold gradation of social rank. In ancient Rome we have patricians, knights, plebeians, slaves; in the Middle Ages, feudal lords, vassals, guild-masters, journeymen, apprentices, serfs; in almost all of these classes, again, subordinate gradations.

The modern bourgeois society that has sprouted from the ruins of feudal society has not done away with class antagonisms. It has but established new classes, new conditions of oppression, new forms of struggle in   20 place of the old ones.

Our epoch, the epoch of the bourgeoisie, possesses, however, this distinctive feature: it has simplified the class antagonisms. Society as a whole is splitting up more and more into two great hostile camps, into two great classes directly facing each other: Bourgeoisie and Proletariat.

From the serfs of the Middle Ages sprang the chartered burghers of the earliest towns. From these burgesses the first elements of the bourgeoisie were   30 developed.

The discovery of America, the rounding of the Cape, opened up fresh ground for the rising bourgeoisie. The East Indian and Chinese markets, the colonization of America, trade with the colonies, the increase in the means of exchange and in commodities generally, gave to commerce, to navigation, to industry, an impulse never before known, and thereby, to the revolutionary element in the tottering feudal society, a rapid development.   40

The feudal system of industry, under which industrial production was monopolized by closed guilds, now no longer sufficed for the growing wants of the new markets. The manufacturing system took its place. The guild-masters were pushed on one side by the manufacturing middle class; division of labor between the different corporate guilds vanished in the face of division of labor in each single workshop.

Meantime the markets kept ever growing, the demand ever rising. Even manufacture no longer   50 sufficed. Thereupon, steam and machinery revolutionized industrial production. The place of manufacture was taken by the giant, Modern Industry, the place of the industrial middle class by industrial millionaires—the leaders of whole industrial armies, the modern bourgeois.

Modern industry has established the world market, for which the discovery of America paved the way. This market has given an immense development to commerce, to navigation, to communication by land.   60 This development has, in its turn, reacted on the extension of industry; and in proportion as industry, commerce, navigation, railways extended, in the same proportion the bourgeoisie developed, increased its capital, and pushed into the background every class handed down from the Middle Ages.

We see, therefore, how the modern bourgeoisie is itself the product of a long course of development, of a series of revolutions in the modes of production and of exchange.   70

Each step in the development of the bourgeoisie was accompanied by a corresponding political advance of that class. An oppressed class under the sway of the feudal nobility, an armed and self-governing association in the medieval commune;[3] here independent urban

---

[1]By bourgeoisie is meant the class of modern capitalists, owners of the means of social production and employers of wage labor. By proletariat, the class of modern wage-laborers who, having no means of production of their own, are reduced to selling their labor power in order to live. [1888].

[2]Guild-master, that is, a full member of a guild, a master within, not a head of a guild. [1888].

---

[3]"Commune" was the name taken in France by the nascent towns even before they had conquered from their feudal lords and masters local self-government and political rights as the "Third Estate." Generally speaking, for the economic development of the bourgeoisie, England is here taken as the typical country; for its political development, France. [1888].

republic (as in Italy and Germany), there taxable "third estate" of the monarchy (as in France), afterward, in the period of manufacture proper, serving either the semi-feudal or the absolute monarchy as a counterpoise against the nobility, and, in fact, cornerstone of the great monarchies in general, the bourgeoisie has at last, since the establishment of Modern Industry and of the world market, conquered for itself, in the modern representative State, exclusive political sway. The executive of the modern State is but a committee for managing the common affairs of the whole bourgeoisie.

The bourgeoisie, historically, has played a most revolutionary part.

The bourgeoisie, wherever it has got the upper hand, has put an end to all feudal, patriarchal, idyllic relations. It has pitilessly torn asunder the motley feudal ties that bound man to his "natural superiors," and has left remaining no other nexus between man and man than naked self-interest, than callous "cash payment." It has drowned the most heavenly ecstasies of religious fervor, of chivalrous enthusiasm, of philistine sentimentalism, in the icy water of egotistical calculation. It has resolved personal worth into exchange value, and in place of the numberless indefeasible chartered freedoms has set up that single, unconscionable freedom—Free Trade. In one word, for exploitation, veiled by religious and political illusions, it has substituted naked, shameless, direct, brutal exploitation.

• The bourgeoisie has stripped of its halo every occupation hitherto honored and looked up to with reverent awe. It has converted the physician, the lawyer, the priest, the poet, the man of science, into its paid wage-laborers.•

• The bourgeoisie has torn away from the family its sentimental veil, and has reduced the family relation to a mere money relation. . . .

The bourgeoisie, by the rapid improvement of all instruments of production, by the immensely facilitated means of communication, draws all, even the most barbarian, nations into civilization. The cheap prices of its commodities are the heavy artillery with which it batters down all Chinese walls, with which it forces the barbarians' intensely obstinate hatred of foreigners to capitulate. It compels all nations, on pain of extinction, to adopt the bourgeois mode of production; it compels them to introduce what it calls civilization into their midst, i.e., to become bourgeois themselves. In a word, it creates a world after its own image. •

The bourgeoisie has subjected the country to the rule of the towns. It has created enormous cities, has greatly increased the urban population as compared with the rural, and has thus rescued a considerable part of the population from the idiocy of rural life. Just as it has made the country dependent on the towns, so it has made barbarian and semi-barbarian countries dependent on the civilized ones, nations of peasants on nations of bourgeois, the East on the West.

The bourgeoisie keeps doing away more and more with the scattered state of the population, of the means of production, and of property. It has agglomerated population, centralized means of production, and has concentrated property in a few hands. The necessary consequence of this was political centralization. Independent or but loosely connected provinces with separate interests, laws, governments and systems of taxation became lumped together into one nation, with one government, one code of laws, one national class interest, one frontier and one customs tariff.

The bourgeoisie during its rule of scarce one hundred years has created more massive and more colossal productive forces than have all preceding generations together. Subjection of nature's forces to man, machinery, application of chemistry to industry and agriculture, steam navigation, railways, electric telegraphs, clearing of whole continents for cultivation, canalization of rivers, whole populations conjured out of the ground—what earlier century had even a presentiment that such productive forces slumbered in the lap of social labor? . . .

But not only has the bourgeoisie forged the weapons that bring death to itself; it has also called into existence the men who are to wield those weapons—the modern working class, the proletarians.

In proportion as the bourgeoisie, i.e., capital, is developed, in the same proportion is the proletariat, the modern working class, developed—a class of laborers who live only as long as they find work, and who find work only as long as their labor increases capital. These laborers, who must sell themselves piecemeal, are a commodity like every other article of commerce, and are consequently exposed to all the vicissitudes of competition, to all the fluctuations of the market.

Owing to the extensive use of machinery and to division of labor, the work of the proletarians has lost all individual character and, consequently, all charm for the workman. He becomes an appendage of the machine, and it is only the most simple, most monotonous, and most easily acquired knack that is required of him. . . .

Modern industry has converted the little workshop of the patriarchal master into the great factory of the industrial capitalist. Masses of laborers, crowded into the factory, are organized like soldiers. As privates of the industrial army they are placed under the command of a perfect hierarchy of officers and sergeants. Not only are they slaves of the bourgeois class and of the bourgeois State; they are daily and hourly enslaved by the machine, by the overseer and, above all, by the individual bourgeois manufacturer himself. The more openly this despotism proclaims gain to be its end and aim, the more petty, the more hateful and the more embittering it is.

• The less the skill and exertion of strength implied in manual labor, in other words, the more modern industry becomes developed, the more is the labor of men superseded by that of women. Differences of age and sex no longer have any distinctive social validity for the working class. All are instruments of labor, more or less expensive to use, according to their age and sex.

No sooner is the exploitation of the laborer by the manufacturer so far at an end that he receives his wages in cash, than he is set upon by the other portions of the bourgeoisie, the landlord, the shopkeeper, the pawnkeeper, etc. . . .

II. Proletarians and Communists

. . . The Communist revolution is the most radical rupture with traditional property relations; no wonder 200 that its development involves the most radical rupture with traditional ideas.

But let us have done with the bourgeois objections to Communism.

We have seen above that the first step in the revolution by the working class is to raise the proletariat to the position of ruling class, to win the battle of democracy.

The proletariat will use its political supremacy to wrest, by degrees, all capital from the bourgeoisie, to 210 centralize all instruments of production in the hands of the State, i.e., of the proletariat organized as the ruling class; and to increase the total of productive forces as rapidly as possible. . . .

III. Position of the Communists

. . . The Communists disdain to conceal their views and aims. They openly declare that their ends can be attained only by the forcible overthrow of all existing social conditions. Let the ruling classes tremble at a Communistic revolution. The proletarians have nothing to lose but their chains. They have a world to win. 220

WORKING MEN OF ALL COUNTRIES, UNITE!

◆

Mill and Women's Rights

While Marx and Engels criticized a society that made middle-class women "mere instrument[s] of production," John Stuart Mill described women of all classes as the unwilling subjects of more powerful males. In the eloquent treatise entitled *The Subjection of Women* (1869), Mill condemned the legal subordination of one sex to the other as objectively "wrong in itself, and . . . one of the chief hindrances to human improvement." Mill's optimism concerning the unbounded potential for social change—a hallmark of liberalism—may have been shortsighted, for women would not obtain voting rights in England until 1928. Nevertheless, in 1837, the first women's college was founded in America, and in 1848, at Seneca Falls in upstate New York, American feminists, led by Elizabeth Cady Stanton (d. 1902) and Susan B. Anthony (d. 1906), issued a declaration that demanded female equality in all areas of life. The

rights of women had been an issue addressed in the literature of feminists from Christine de Pisan to Condorcet and Mary Wollstonecroft, but nowhere was the plight of women more eloquently treated than in Mill's essay. Mill compared the subjection of women to that of other subject classes in the history of culture. But his most original contribution was his analysis of the male/female relationship and his explanation of how that relationship differed from that of master and slave.

READING 105 From Mill's *The Subjection of Women*

All causes, social and natural, combine to make it unlikely that women should be collectively rebellious to the power of men. They are so far in a position different from all other subject classes that their masters require something more from them than actual service. Men do not want solely the obedience of women, they want their sentiments. All men, except the most brutish, desire to have, in the woman most nearly connected with them, not a forced slave but a willing one, not a slave merely, but a favorite. They have therefore put everything in 10 practice to enslave their minds. The masters of all other slaves rely, for maintaining obedience, on fear, either fear of themselves, or religious fears. The masters of women wanted more than simple obedience, and they turned the whole force of education to effect their purpose. All women are brought up from the very earliest years in the belief that their ideal of character is the very opposite to that of men; not self-will and government by self-control, but submission and yielding to the control of others. All the moralities tell them that it 20 is the duty of women and all the current sentimentalities that it is their nature to live for others, to make complete abnegation of themselves, and to have no life but in their affections. And by their affections are meant the only ones they are allowed to have—those to the men with whom they are connected, or to the children who constitute an additional and indefeasible tie between them and a man. When we put together three things— first, the natural attraction between opposite sexes; secondly, the wife's entire dependence on the husband, 30 every privilege or pleasure she has being either his gift, or depending entirely on his will; and lastly, that the principal object of human pursuit, consideration, and all objects of social ambition can in general be sought or obtained by her only through him, it would be a miracle if the object of being attractive to men had not become the polar star of feminine education and formation of character. And this great means of influence over the minds of women having been acquired, an instinct of selfishness made men avail themselves of it to the 40 utmost as a means of holding women in subjection, by representing to them meekness, submissiveness, and resignation of all individual will into the hands of a man, as an essential part of sexual attractiveness. . . . •

The preceding considerations are amply sufficient to show that custom, however universal it may be, affords in this case no presumption and ought not to create any prejudice in favor of the arrangements which place women in social and political subjection to men. But I may go further, and maintain that the course of history, and the tendencies of progressive human society afford not only no presumption in favor of this system of inequality of rights, but a strong one against it; and that, so far as the whole course of human improvement up to this time, the whole stream of modern tendencies warrants any inference on the subject, it is that this relic of the past is discordant with the future and must necessarily disappear.

For, what is the peculiar character of the modern world—the difference which chiefly distinguishes modern institutions, modern social ideas, modern life itself, from those of times long past? It is, that human beings are no longer born to their place in life and chained down by an inexorable bond to the place they are born to, but are free to employ their faculties and such favorable chances as offer, to achieve the lot which may appear to them most desirable. Human society of old was constituted on a very different principle. All were born to a fixed social position and were mostly kept in it by law or interdicted from any means by which they could emerge from it. As some men are born white and others black, so some were born slaves and others freemen and citizens; some were born patricians, others plebeians; some were born feudal nobles, others commoners. . . .

The old theory was that the least possible should be left to the choice of the individual agent; that all he had to do should, as far as practicable, be laid down for him by superior wisdom. Left to himself he was sure to go wrong. The modern conviction, the fruit of a thousand years of experience, is that things in which the individual is the person directly interested never go right but as they are left to his own discretion; and that any regulation of them by authority, except to protect the rights of others, is sure to be mischievous. . . .

50

60

70

80

———————◆———————

Realism in Literature

The Novels of Dickens and Twain

Inequities of class and gender had existed throughout the course of history, but in an age that pitted the progressive effects of industrial capitalism against the realities of poverty and inequality, social criticism was inevitable. Nineteenth-century writers pointed to these conditions and described them with unembellished objectivity. This unblinking attention to contemporary life and experience was the basis for the style known as *literary realism.*

More than any other genre, the nineteenth-century novel—by its capacity to detail characters and conditions—best fulfilled the realist credo of depicting life with complete candor. In contrast with romanticism, which embraced heroic and exotic subjects, realists portrayed men and women in actual, everyday situations. They examined the social consequences of middle-class materialism, the plight of the working class, and the subjugation of women, among other matters. While realism never totally displaced romanticism as the dominant literary mode of the nineteenth century, it often appeared alongside the romantic—indeed, romantic and sentimental elements might be found in generally realistic portrayals of life. Such was the case in the novels of Charles Dickens (d. 1870) in England and Mark Twain, a pseudonym of Samuel Longhorne Clemens (d. 1910), in America. Twain's writings, including his greatest achievement, *The Adventures of Huckleberry Finn* (1884), reveal a blend of humor and irony that is not generally characteristic of Dickens. But both writers employed a masterful use of dialect, sensitivity to pictorial detail, and a humanitarian sympathy in their descriptions of nineteenth-century life in specific locales—for Twain, the rural farmlands along the Mississippi River, and for Dickens, the streets of England's industrial cities.

Dickens, the most popular English novelist of his time, came from a poor family that provided him with little formal education. His early experiences supplied some of the themes for his most famous novels: *Oliver Twist* (1839) vividly portrays the slums, orphanages, and boarding schools of London; *Nicholas Nickleby* (1839) is a bitter indictment of England's brutal rural schools; and *David Copperfield* (1850) condemns debtor's prisons and the conditions that produced them. Dickens' novels are frequently theatrical, his characters may be drawn to the point of caricature, and his themes often suggest a sentimental faith in kindness and good cheer as the best antidotes to the bitterness of contemporary life. But, as the following excerpt illustrates, Dickens' grasp of realistic detail was acute, and his portrayal of physical ugliness was unflinching. In this passage from *The Old Curiosity Shop* (1841), Dickens painted an unforgettable picture of the horrifying urban conditions that gave rise to the despair of the laboring classes and inspired their cries for social reform. Dickens' description of the English milltown of Birmingham, as first viewed by the novel's heroine, little Nell, and her grandfather, finds striking parallels in nineteenth-century visual representations of Europe's laboring poor (figure 30.3); it also calls to mind the popular conceptions of Hell found in medieval art and literature (figures 12.1 and 12.3).

READING 106 From Dickens' *Old Curiosity Shop*

● A long suburb of red-brick houses—some with patches of garden-ground, where coal-dust and factory smoke darkened the shrinking leaves and coarse, rank flowers; and where the struggling vegetation sickened and sank under the hot breath of kiln and furnace, making them by its presence seem yet more blighting and unwholesome than in the town itself—a long, flat, straggling suburb passed, they came by slow degrees upon a cheerless region, where not a blade of grass was seen to grow; where not a bud put forth its promise   10
in the spring; where nothing green could live but on the surface of the stagnant pools, which here and there lay idly sweltering by the black roadside. ●

Advancing more and more into the shadow of this mournful place, its dark depressing influence stole upon their spirits, and filled them with a dismal gloom. On every side, and far as the eye could see into the heavy distance, tall chimneys, crowding on each other, and presenting that endless repetition of the same dull, ugly form, which in the horror of oppressive dreams, poured   20
out their plague of smoke, obscured the light, and made foul the melancholy air. On mounds of ashes by the wayside, sheltered only by a few rough boards, or rotten pent-house roofs, strange engines spun and writhed like tortured creatures; clanking their iron chains, shrieking in their rapid whirl from time to time as though in torment unendurable, and making the ground tremble with their agonies. Dismantled houses here and there

appeared, tottering to the earth, propped up by fragments of others that had fallen down, unroofed,   30
windowless, blackened, desolate, but yet inhabited. Men, women, children, wan in their looks and ragged in attire, tended the engines, fed their tributary fires, begged upon the road, or scowled half naked from the doorless houses. Then came more of the wrathful monsters, whose like they almost seemed to be in their wildness and their untamed air, screeching and turning round and round again; and still, before, behind, and to the right and left, was the same interminable perspective of brick towers, never ceasing in their black   40
vomit, blasting all things living or inanimate, shutting out the face of day, and closing in on all these horrors with a dense dark cloud.

● But night-time in this dreadful spot!—night, when the smoke was changed to fire; when every chimney spirted up its flame; and places, that had been dark vaults all day, now shone red-hot, with figures moving to and fro within their blazing jaws, and calling to one another with hoarse cries—night, when the noise of every strange machine was aggravated by the darkness; when the   50
people near them looked wilder and more savage; when bands of unemployed laborers paraded in the roads, or clustered by torch-light round their leaders, who told them in stern language of their wrongs, and urged them on to frightful cries and threats; when maddened men, armed with sword and firebrand, spurning the tears and prayers of women who would restrain them, rushed forth on errands of terror and destruction, to work no ruin half so surely as their own—night, when carts came rumbling by, filled with rude coffins (for contagious   60
disease and death had been busy with the living crops); when orphans cried, and distracted women shrieked and followed in their wake—night, when some called for bread, and some for drink to drown their cares; and some with tears, and some with staggering feet, and some with bloodshot eyes, went brooding home—night, which, unlike the night that Heaven sends on earth, brought with it no peace, nor quiet, nor signs of blessed sleep—who shall tell the terrors of the night to that young wandering child! ●   70

———————————◆———————————

The Novels of Dostoevsky and Tolstoy

Even more pessimistic than Dickens, and more profoundly analytic of the universal human condition, were the Russian novelists Fyodor Dostoevsky (d. 1881) and Leo Tolstoy (d. 1910). Both men were born and bred in wealth, but both turned against the decadence of upper-class Russian society and sympathized with the plight of the lower classes. Tolstoy ultimately renounced his wealth and property and went to live and work among the peasants. Tolstoy's historical novel *War and Peace* (1869), often hailed as the greatest example of realistic Russian fiction, traces the progress of five families whose destinies unroll against the background of Napoleon's invasion of Russia in 1812. In this sprawling narrative, as in many of his other novels, Tolstoy exposes the privileged position of the nobility and the cruel exploitation of the great masses of Russian people.

While Tolstoy's novels focus on the habits and struggles of Russia's various classes, Dostoevsky's generally address psychological issues. The characters in Dostoevsky's novels, like Dostoevsky himself, are often victims of a dual plight: poverty and conscience. Their energies are foiled by the struggle to resolve their own contradictory passions. Such novels as *Crime and Punishment* (1866), *The Possessed* (1871), and *The Brothers Karamazov* (1880)—Dostoevsky's most compelling work—feature introspective characters whose psychological malaise becomes the central theme of the novel.

The Novels of Flaubert

Nineteenth-century French novelists shared with British, American, and Russian realists an interest in the ways in which society shapes and determines the personality. The characters in the novels of the French writer Gustave Flaubert (d. 1880) do not create the world in their own image; rather, the world—or more specifically, the social and economic environment—molds them and governs their destinies. Flaubert, whom critics have called "the inventor of the modern novel," stripped his novels of sentimentality and of all preconceived notions of behavior. He aimed at a precise description of not only the stuff of the physical world but also the psychological states of his characters.

Flaubert's most famous novel, *Madame Bovary,* tells the story of a middle-class woman who desperately seeks to escape the boredom of her mundane existence. Educated in the convent and married to a dull, small-town physician, Emma Bovary tries to live out the fantasies that fill the pages of her favorite romance novels, but her efforts to do so prove disastrous and lead to her ultimate destruction. Flaubert reconstructs with a minimum of interpretation the details of Emma's provincial surroundings and her bleak marriage. A meticulous observer, he sought *le mot juste* ("the precise word") to describe each concrete object and each psychological state—a practice that often prevented him from writing more than one or two pages of prose per week. Since the novel achieves its full effect through the gradual development of plot and character, no brief excerpt can possibly do it justice. Nevertheless, the following three paragraphs from *Madame Bovary* illustrate Flaubert's ability to characterize places and persons by means of the fastidious selection of realistic details. The mundane particulars of this descriptive passage convey the staleness and inescapability of nineteenth-century French provincial life and the futility of Emma's personal despair.

READING 107 From Flaubert's *Madame Bovary*

Every day at the same time the schoolmaster in his black silk skullcap opened the shutters of his house; every day at the same time the village policeman passed, his sword buckled around his smock. Morning and evening the post horses crossed the road in threes to drink at the pond. Now and again the bell of a café door would tinkle as it opened; and when there was a wind she could hear the little copper basins that formed the barber's shop-sign creaking on their two rods. His window display consisted of an old fashion plate stuck on one of the panes, and a wax bust of a woman with yellow hair. The barber, too, was accustomed to bewail[ing] the waste of his talents, his ruined career; and dreaming of a shop in a large city—in Rouen, perhaps, on the river front, or near the theatre—he paced back and forth all day between the mayor's office and the church, gloomily waiting for customers. When Madame Bovary raised her eyes she always saw him there with his cap over one ear, and his short work jacket, like a sentry on duty.

In the afternoon, sometimes, a man's face appeared outside the parlor windows, a swarthy face with black side whiskers and slow, wide, gentle smile that showed very white teeth. Then would come the strain of a waltz; and in a miniature drawing room on top of the hurdy-gurdy a set of tiny dancers would begin to revolve. Women in pink turbans, Tyrolians in jackets, monkeys in black tailcoats, gentlemen in knee breeches—they all spun around among the armchairs, sofas and tables, and were reflected in bits of mirror glass joined together at the edges by strips of gold paper. As he turned his

10

20

30

crank the man would glance to his right, to his left, and toward the windows. Now and then he would let out a spurt of brown saliva against the curb and raise his knee to lift the instrument and ease the heavy shoulder strap; and the music, now doleful and dragging, now merry and quick, came out of the box through a pink taffeta curtain under a fancy brasswork grill. The tunes it played were tunes that were being heard in other places—in theatres, in drawing rooms, under the lighted 40 chandeliers of ballrooms: echoes from the world that reached Emma this way. Sarabands ran on endlessly in her head; and her thoughts, like dancing girls on some flowery carpet, leapt with the notes from dream to dream, from sorrow to sorrow. Then, when the man had caught in his cap the coin she threw him, he would pull down an old blue wool cover, hoist his organ onto his back, and move heavily off. She always watched him till he disappeared.

• But it was above all at mealtime that she could bear 50 it no longer—in that small ground-floor room with its smoking stove, its squeaking door, its sweating walls and its damp floor tiles. All the bitterness of life seemed to be served up to her on her plate; and the steam rising from the boiled meat brought gusts of revulsion from the depths of her soul. Charles was a slow eater; she would nibble a few hazelnuts, or lean on her elbow and draw lines on the oilcloth with the point of her table knife. . . .•

Zola and the Naturalistic Novel

Flaubert's contemporary, Émile Zola (d. 1902), initiated a variant form of literary realism, known as *naturalism*. Like realism, naturalist fiction was based on the premise that life should be represented objectively and without embellishment or idealization. But naturalists differed from realists in taking a deterministic approach that showed human beings as products of environmental or hereditary factors over which they had little or no control. Just as Marx held that economic life shaped all aspects of culture, so naturalists believed that material and social elements determined human conduct. In his passion to describe the world with absolute fidelity, Zola amassed notebooks filled with information on a wide variety of subjects, including coal mining, the railroads, the stock market, and the science of surgery. Zola treated the novel as an exact study of commonplace, material existence. He presented a slice of life that showed how social and material circumstances influenced human behavior. His subjects were as brutally uncompromising as his style. *The Grog Shop* (1877) offered a terrifying picture of the effects of alcoholism on industrial workers; *Germinal* (1885) exposed the bitter lives of

French coal miners; and his most scandalous novel, *Nana* (1880), was a scathing portrayal of a beautiful but unscrupulous prostitute.

Strong elements of naturalism are found in the novels of many late nineteenth-century writers in both Europe and America. Thomas Hardy (d. 1916) in England, and Stephen Crane (d. 1900), Jack London (d. 1916), and Theodore Dreiser (d. 1945) in America are the most notable of the English-language literary naturalists.

The Plays of Ibsen

The Norwegian dramatist Henrik Ibsen (d. 1906) brought to the late nineteenth-century stage concerns similar to those that appeared in the novels of the European and American realists. A moralist and a student of human behavior, Ibsen rebelled against the artificial social conventions that led people to pursue self-deluding and hypocritical lives. Ibsen was deeply concerned with contemporary issues and social problems. He shocked the public by writing prose dramas that addressed such controversial subjects as insanity, incest, and venereal disease. At the same time, he explored universal themes of conflict between the individual and society, between love and duty, and between husband and wife.

In 1879, Ibsen wrote the classic drama of female liberation, *A Doll's House*. The play traces the awakening of a middle-class woman to the meaninglessness of her role as "a doll-wife" living in "a doll's house." Threatened by blackmail over a debt she incurred years earlier, Nora Helmer looks to her priggish, egotistical husband, Torvald, for protection. When he fails to provide that protection, Nora realizes she must discard her dependent life-style. She comes to recognize that her first obligation is to herself and to her dignity as a reasonable human being. Nora's revelation brings to life, in the forceful language of everyday speech, the psychological tension between male and female that Mill had analyzed only years earlier in his treatise on the subjection of women. Ibsen does not resolve the question of whether a woman's duties to husband and children come before her duty to herself; yet, as is suggested in the following exchange between Nora and Torvald (excerpted from the last scene of *A Doll's House*), Nora's self-discovery precipitates the end of her marriage. Nora shuts the door on the illusions of the past as emphatically as Ibsen—a half-century after Goethe's *Faust*—may be said to have turned his back on the world of romantic idealism.

Act III, Final Scene

[*Late at night in the Helmer's living room. Instead of retiring, Nora suddenly appears in street clothes.*]

● **Helmer:** . . . What's all this? I thought you were going to bed. You've changed your dress?

Nora: Yes, Torvald; I've changed my dress.

Helmer: But what for? At this hour?

Nora: I shan't sleep tonight.

Helmer: But, Nora dear—

Nora: [*looking at her watch*]: It's not so very late—Sit down, Torvald; we have a lot to talk about.

[*She sits at one side of the table.*]

Helmer: Nora—what does this mean? Why that stern expression?   10

Nora: Sit down. It'll take some time. I have a lot to say to you.

[*Helmer sits at the other side of the table.*]

Helmer: You frighten me, Nora. I don't understand you.

Nora: No, that's just it. You don't understand me; and I have never understood you either—until tonight. No, don't interrupt me. Just listen to what I have to say. This is to be a final settlement, Torvald.   20

Helmer: How do you mean?

Nora: [*after a short silence*]: Doesn't anything special strike you as we sit here like this?

Helmer: I don't think so—why?

Nora: It doesn't occur to you, does it, that though we've been married for eight years, this is the first time that we two—man and wife—have sat down for a serious talk?

Helmer: What do you mean by serious?

Nora: During eight whole years, no—more than   30 that—ever since the first day we met—we have never exchanged so much as one serious word about serious things.

Helmer: Why should I perpetually burden you with all my cares and problems? How could you possibly help me to solve them?

Nora: I'm not talking about cares and problems. I'm simply saying we've never once sat down seriously and tried to get to the bottom of anything.

Helmer: But, Nora, darling—why should you be   40 concerned with serious thoughts?

Nora: That's the whole point! You've never understood me—A great injustice has been done me, Torvald; first by Father, and then by you.

Helmer: What a thing to say! No two people on earth could ever have loved you more than we have!

Nora: [*shaking her head*]: You never loved me. You just thought it was fun to be in love with me.

Helmer: This is fantastic!

Nora: Perhaps. But it's true all the same. While I   50 was still at home I used to hear Father airing his opinions and they became my opinions; or if I didn't happen to agree, I kept it to myself—he would have been displeased otherwise. He used to call me his doll-baby, and played with me as I played with my dolls. Then I came to live in your house—

Helmer: What an expression to use about our marriage!

Nora: [*undisturbed*]: I mean—from Father's hands I passed into yours. You arranged everything according   60 to your tastes, and I acquired the same tastes, or I pretended to—I'm not sure which—a little of both, perhaps. Looking back on it all, it seems to me I've lived here like a beggar, from hand to mouth. I've lived by performing tricks for you, Torvald. But that's the way you wanted it. You and Father have done me a great wrong. You've prevented me from becoming a real person.

Helmer: Nora, how can you be so ungrateful and unreasonable! Haven't you been happy here?   70

Nora: No, never. I thought I was; but I wasn't really.

Helmer: Not—not happy!

Nora: No, only merry. You've always been so kind to me. But our home has never been anything but a play-room. I've been your doll-wife, just as at home I was Papa's doll-child. And the children in turn, have been my dolls. I thought it fun when you played games with me, just as they thought it fun when I played games with them. And that's been our marriage, Torvald.

Helmer: There may be a grain of truth in what you   80 say, even though it is distorted and exaggerated. From now on things will be different. Play-time is over now; tomorrow lessons begin!

Nora: Whose lessons? Mine, or the children's?

Helmer: Both, if you wish it, Nora, dear.

Nora: Torvald, I'm afraid you're not the man to teach me to be a real wife to you.

Helmer: How can you say that?

Nora: And I'm certainly not fit to teach the children.

Helmer: Nora!   90

Nora: Didn't you just say, a moment ago, you didn't dare trust them to me?

Helmer: That was in the excitement of the moment! You mustn't take it so seriously!

Nora: But you were quite right, Torvald. That job is beyond me; there's another job I must do first: I must try and educate myself. You could never help me to do that; I must do it quite alone. So, you see—that's why I'm going to leave you.

Helmer: [*jumping up*]: What did you say—?   100

Nora: I shall never get to know myself—I shall never learn to face reality—unless I stand alone. So I can't stay with you any longer.

Helmer: Nora! Nora!

Nora: I am going at once. I'm sure Kristine will let me stay with her tonight—

Helmer: But, Nora—this is madness! I shan't allow you to do this. I shall forbid it!

Nora: You no longer have the power to forbid me anything. I'll only take a few things with me—those that belong to me. I shall never again accept anything from you. 110

Helmer: Have you lost your senses?

Nora: Tomorrow I'll go home—to what *was* my home, I mean. It might be easier for me there, to find something to do.

Helmer: You talk like an ignorant child, Nora—!

Nora: Yes. That's just why I must educate myself.

Helmer: To leave your home—to leave your husband, and your children! What do you suppose people would say to that? 120

Nora: It makes no difference. This is something I *must* do.

Helmer: It's inconceivable! Don't you realize you'd be betraying your most sacred duty?

Nora: What do you consider that to be?

Helmer: Your duty towards your husband and your children—I surely don't have to tell you that!

Nora: I've another duty just as sacred.

Helmer: Nonsense! What duty do you mean? 130

Nora: My duty towards myself.

Helmer: Remember—before all else you are a wife and mother.

Nora: I don't believe that anymore. I believe that before all else I am a human being, just as you are—or at least that I should try and become one. I know that most people would agree with you, Torvald—and that's what they say in books. But I can no longer be satisfied with what most people say—or what they write in books. I must think things out for myself—get clear 140 about them.

Helmer: Surely your position in your home is clear enough? Have you no sense of religion? Isn't that an infallible guide to you?

Nora: But don't you see, Torvald—I don't really know what religion is.

Helmer: Nora! How *can* you!

Nora: All I know about it is what Pastor Hansen told me when I was confirmed. He taught me what he thought religion was—said it was *this* and *that*. As soon 150 as I get away by myself, I shall have to look into that matter too, try and decide whether what he taught me was right—or whether it's right for *me,* at least.

Helmer: A nice way for a young woman to talk! It's unheard of! If religion means nothing to you, I'll appeal to your conscience; you must have some sense of ethics, I suppose? Answer me! Or have you none?

Nora: It's hard for me to answer you, Torvald. I don't think I know—all these things bewilder me. But I *do* know that I think quite differently from you about them. 160 I've discovered that the law, for instance, is quite different from what I had imagined; but I find it hard to believe it can be right. It seems it's criminal for a woman to try and spare her old, sick, father, or save her husband's life! I can't agree with that.

Helmer: You talk like a child. You have no understanding of the society we live in.

Nora: No, I haven't. But I'm going to try and learn. I want to find out which of us is right—society or I.

Helmer: You are ill, Nora; you have a touch of fever; 170 you're quite beside yourself.

Nora: I've never felt so sure—so clear-headed—as I do tonight.

Helmer: "Sure and clear-headed" enough to leave your husband and your children?

Nora: Yes.

Helmer: Then there is only one explanation possible.

Nora: What?

Helmer: You don't love me any more. 180

Nora: No; that is just it.

Helmer: Nora!—What are you saying!

Nora: It makes me so unhappy, Torvald; for you've always been so kind to me. But I can't help it. I don't love you any more.

Helmer: [*mastering himself with difficulty*]: You feel "sure and clear-headed" about this too?

Nora: Yes, utterly sure. That's why I can't stay here any longer.

. . . .

—————◆—————

Realism in the Visual Arts

The Birth of Photography

One of the most significant factors in the development of the realist mentality was the birth of photography. Photography, literally "writing with light," had its beginnings in 1839, when the French inventor Louis J. M. Daguerre (d. 1851) successfully exposed a light-sensitive metal plate and fixed the image with common chemicals. Gradual improvements in camera lenses and in the chemicals used to develop the visible image hastened the rise of photography as a popular device for recording the physical world with unprecedented accuracy. And while photographers, like other artists, might exercise subjectivity in their choice of subject matter, they quickly established themselves as masters of unvarnished realism.

By mid-century, photographers were using the camera for a wide variety of purposes: they made topographical studies, recorded architectural monuments, and produced thousands of portrait images.

FIGURE 30.4 **Dead Confederate Soldier with Gun, Mathew B. Brady or staff, Petersburg, Virginia, 1865. Photograph. The Library of Congress, Washington, D.C.**

FIGURE 30.5 *Whisper of the Muse,* Julia Margaret Cameron, *G. F. Watts and Children,* ca. 1865. Photograph. Collection The Royal Photographic Society, Bath.

The documentary photographs of the American Civil War (1861–65) produced by Mathew B. Brady (d. 1896) and his staff demonstrated the importance of the photographer as a chronicler of human life. While a painting or engraving might bring to life the content of the artist's imagination, a photograph offered an authentic record of a moment vanished in time. Brady's thirty-five hundred Civil War photographs included mundane scenes of barracks and munitions as well as unflinching views of human carnage (figure 30.4). Discounting the camera's obvious challenge to the role of the artist as recorder and interpreter of the visual world, nineteenth-century artists explored the aesthetic potential of the new medium. Many European and American painters made photographic studies and used photographs as factual models for their paintings. At the same time, the pioneer photographer Julia Margaret Cameron (d. 1879) employed the camera to imitate the effects of the brush. Cameron's soft-focus portraits were distinctly romantic in spirit (figure 30.5).

FIGURE 30.6 *The Stone-Breakers,* **Gustave Courbet, 1849. Approx. 5 ft. 5 in. × 7 ft. 10 in. Gemäldegalerie Abt. Neue Meister, Staatliche Kunstsammlungen, Dresden. (Painting lost during World War II.) Photo: Sächsische Landesbibliothck, Dresden.**

Courbet and French Realist Painting

In late nineteenth-century painting no less than in literature, realism flourished alongside romanticism. The realist preference for concrete, matter-of-fact depictions of everyday life provided a sober alternative to both the romantic taste for remote, exotic, and heroic imagery and the neoclassical love of noble and elevated themes. Obedient to the credo that artists must confront the experiences and appearances of their own time, realist painters abandoned the nostalgic landscapes and heroic themes of romantic art in favor of scenes that showed the consequences of industrialism (figure 30.2) and the lives of ordinary men and women.

The leading realist of nineteenth-century French painting was Gustave Courbet (d. 1877). A farmer's son, Courbet was a self-taught artist, an outspoken socialist, and a staunch defender of the realist cause. "A painter," he protested, "should paint only what he can see." Indeed, most of Courbet's works—portraits, landscapes, and contemporary scenes—remain true to the tangible facts of his immediate vision. With the challenge "Show me an angel and I'll paint one," he taunted both the romantics and the neoclassicists. Not angels but ordinary individuals in their actual settings and circumstances interested Courbet.

In *The Stone-Breakers* of 1849, Courbet depicted two rural laborers performing the most menial of physical tasks (figure 30.6). The painting, which Courbet's friend Proudhon called "the first socialist picture," outraged the critics because its subject matter was mundane and its figures were crude, ragged, and totally unidealized. Moreover, the figures were positioned with their backs turned toward the

FIGURE 30.7 *The Gleaners,* Jean Francois Millet, ca. 1857. Black conte crayon on paper, approx. 6 7/8 in. × 10 3/8 in. The George A. Lucas Collection of The Maryland Institute, College of Art, on indefinite loan to the Baltimore Museum of Art BMA L 1933.53.5

viewer, thus violating, by nineteenth-century standards, the rules of propriety and decorum enshrined in French academic art (chapter 23). Despite such "violations" Courbet's painting appealed to the masses. In a country whose population was still two-thirds rural and largely poor, the stolid dignity of hard labor was a popular subject, so popular, in fact, that it was often romanticized. A comparison of *The Stone-Breakers* with a study by Jean François Millet for his painting *The Gleaners* (figure 30.7) illustrates the difference between Courbet's undiluted realism and Millet's romanticized realism. Millet's workers are as ordinary and anonymous as Courbet's, but they are also dignified and graceful, betraying a distant kin-

ship with Raphael's heroic figures (figure 17.23). Whereas Courbet's workers seem trapped behind the narrow roadside bank, Millet's dominate a broad and ennobling vista. And while Courbet's scene has the "random" and accidental look of a snapshot, Millet's composition—in which the contours of haystacks and wagon delicately answer the curved backs of the laborers—observes the traditional academic precepts of balance and formal design. Millet removed nature's "flaws" and imposed the imagination upon the immediate evidence of the senses. His romanticized views of the laboring classes became some of the best-loved images of the nineteenth century. Courbet, however, remained brutally loyal to nature.

FIGURE 30.8 *Burial at Ornans,* Gustave Courbet, 1849–50. Oil on canvas, approx. 10 ft. 3 in. × 21 ft. 9 in. Louvre, Paris. Cliché des Musées Nationaux, Paris. © Photo R.M.N.

Courbet's *Burial at Ornans* was his most daring and monumental effort to portray ordinary life in an unembellished manner. The huge canvas (over 21 by 10 feet) consists of fifty-two life-size figures shown witnessing a somber, small-town burial (figure 30.8). Traditional representations of death and burial usually gave prominence to the trappings of Christian ritual, but in this painting, Courbet ignored all pomp and ceremony. The kneeling gravedigger and the attendant dog are as important to the pictorial statement as are the priest and his retinue, and the mourners command more interest than the deceased, whose body is omitted from view. With the objectivity of a camera eye, Courbet captured the factual and renounced sentimentality and artifice.

Social Realism in the Art of Daumier

The French artist Honoré Daumier (d. 1879) left a detailed record of the social life of his time. A foremost draftsman, Daumier's favorite technique was **lithography**—a printmaking process created by drawing on a stone plate (figure 30.9). Lithography, a product of nineteenth-century technology, was a cheap and popular means of providing illustrations for newspapers, magazines, and books (figure 28.3). During his lifetime, Daumier produced over four thousand lithographs, often turning out two to three per week for distribution by various Paris newspapers and journals.

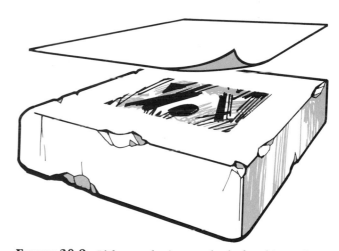

FIGURE 30.9 Lithography is a method of making prints from a flat surface; also called planography. An image is first drawn or painted with an oil-based lithographic crayon or pencil on a smooth limestone surface. The surface is wiped with water, which will not stick to the applied areas of greasy lithographic ink because oil and water do not mix. The greasy areas resist the water and are thus exposed. The surface is then rolled with printing ink, which adheres only to the parts drawn in the oil-based medium. Dampened paper is placed over the stone, and a special flatbed press rubs the back of the paper, transferring the work from the stone to the covering sheet.

FIGURE 30.10 *Nadar Raising Photography to the Heights of Art,* Honoré Daumier, 1862. Lithograph. The balloonist, photographer, draftsman, and journalist Félix Tournachon, called Nadar, took his first photograph from a balloon. Historical Pictures Service, Inc., Chicago.

For his subject matter, Daumier turned directly to the world around him—the streets of Paris, the theater, and the law courts. The activities of Gaspard Felix Tournachon (d. 1910), called Nadar, a pioneer in aerial photography, attracted Daumier's attention (figure 30.10), as did many other modern wonders, such as the telegraph, the sewing machine, the repeating rifle, the railroad, the wire petticoat, and urban renewal projects that included widening the streets of Paris. Daumier did not simply depict the facts of modern life; he poked fun at them. Skeptical as to whether the new technology could radically alter the human condition, he drew attention to characteristic human weaknesses, from the hypocrisy of lawyers and the pretensions of the *nouveau riche* to the pompous and all too familiar complacency of self-serving officials (figure 30.11). The ancestors of modern-day political cartoons, many of Daumier's lithographs reflect his bitter opposition to monarchy, political corruption, and profiteering. Such criticism did not go unnoticed: for publishing a lithograph that showed the French king Louis Philippe as a gluttonous Gargantua, sitting upon a commode/throne and defecating bags of gold, Daumier was promptly thrown in jail.

FIGURE 30.11 *Le Ventre Législatif (The Legislative Belly),* Honoré Daumier, 1834. Lithograph, 11 in. × 17 in. Arizona State University Art Collections, Arizona State University, Tempe, Arizona, gift of Oliver B. James.

FIGURE 30.12 *The Third-Class Carriage,* Honoré Daumier, ca. 1862. Oil on canvas, 25 3/4 in. × 35 1/2 in. The Metropolitan Museum of Art, Bequest of Mrs. H. O. Havemeyer, 1929, The H.O. Havemeyer Collection.

Primarily a graphic artist, Daumier completed fewer than three hundred paintings. In *The Third-Class Carriage,* however, he captured on canvas the shabby monotony of nineteenth-century lower-class railway travel (figure 30.12). The part of the European train in which tickets were the least expensive was also, of course, the least comfortable: it lacked glass windows (hence was subject to more than average amounts of smoke, cinders, and clatter) and was equipped with hard wooden benches rather than cushioned seats. Three generations of poor folk—an elderly woman, a younger woman, and her children—occupy the foreground of Daumier's painting. Their lumpish bodies suggest weariness and futility but yet, a humble dignity reminiscent of Rembrandt's figures (figure 21.3). Dark and loosely sketched oil glazes underscore the mood of cheerless resignation. Daumier conceived a forthright image of common humanity in a contemporary urban setting.

The Scandalous Realism of Manet

As in the prose of Dickens, Tolstoy, and Ibsen, so in the paintings of Edouard Manet (d. 1883) realism challenged tradition. Manet was an admirer of the art of the old masters, especially Velásquez, but he was equally enthralled by the life of his own time—by Parisians and their middle-class pleasures. No less than Ibsen, Manet shocked the public by recasting traditional subjects in modern guise. In a large canvas of 1863 entitled *Déjeuner sur l'herbe (Luncheon on the Grass),* he depicted a nude woman calmly enjoying a picnic lunch with two fully clothed men, while a second, partially clothed woman bathes in a nearby stream (figure 30.13). While Manet's subject matter— the nude in a landscape—was quite traditional (see Giorgione, figure 17.31, and Boucher, figure 26.8), and

FIGURE 30.13 *Déjeuner sur l'herbe,* Edouard Manet, 1863. Oil on canvas, 7 ft. × 8 ft. 10 in. The Jeu de Paume, Paris, Cliché des Musées Nationaux, Paris. Photo: © R.M.N.

FIGURE 30.14 Detail from *The Judgement of Paris,* Marcantonio Raimondi, ca. 1520. Engraving after Raphael tapestry. © Giraudon/Art Resource, New York.

some of his motifs were borrowed from a sixteenth-century engraving of a Raphael tapestry (figure 30.14), Manet's figures carried no noble classical or allegorical message. They were neither woodland nymphs nor Olympian gods and goddesses but ordinary people—Manet's favorite female model, Victorine Meurent (in the nude), and his future brother-in-law (the reclining male figure).

Déjeuner was one of four thousand paintings rejected by the official organ of French art, the jury of the Royal Academy. Nevertheless, it was displayed in 1863 at the *Salon des Refusés* ("the Salon of the Rejected Painters"), a landmark exhibition authorized by the French head of state in response to public agitation against the tyranny of the academy. No sooner was Manet's painting hung, however, than visitors tried to poke holes in the canvas and critics began to attack its coarse "improprieties." If, in the manner of

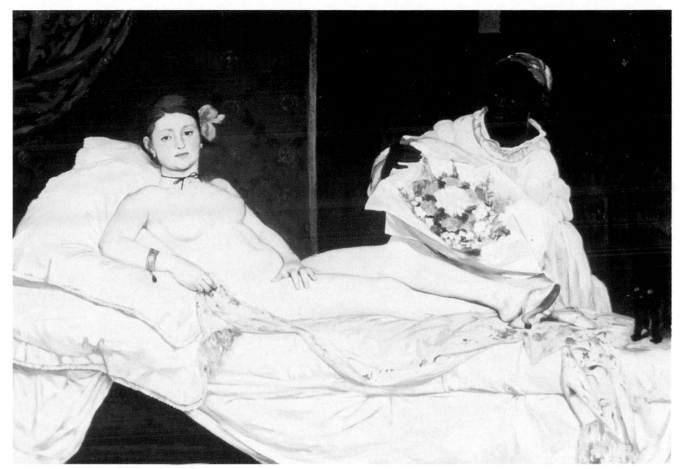

FIGURE 30.15 *Olympia,* Edouard Manet, 1863. Oil on canvas, 51 1/4 in. × 74 3/4 in. The Jeu de Paume, Paris, Cliché des Musées Nationaux, Paris. © Photo R.M.N.

academic artists, Manet had painted a company of nude and semiclothed gods and goddesses romping in the hills of Arcadia, the painting might have been well-received; but, as a representation of Manet's own friends sitting in a Paris park, *Déjeuner* was pronounced scandalous. Critics also attacked Manet's inelegant style: one wrote, "The nude does not have a good figure, and one cannot imagine anything uglier than the man stretched out beside her, who has not even thought of removing, out of doors, his horrible padded cap."

In a second painting completed in 1863, *Olympia,* Manet again "debased" a traditional subject—the reclining nude (figure 30.15). The short, stocky Olympia (Victorine again), stares at the viewer boldly and with none of the subtle allure of a Titian Venus or an Ingres Odalisque. Her satin slippers and the enticing black ribbon at her throat distinguish her as a courtesan rather than a goddess. One contemporary newspaper critic called *Olympia* "a sort of female gorilla" and

warned, "Truly, young girls and women about to become mothers would do well, if they are wise, to run away from this spectacle." Like Flaubert's *Madame Bovary* or Zola's *Nana,* Manet's *Olympia* desentimentalized the image of the female. By deflating the ideal and rendering reality in commonplace terms, Manet not only offended public taste, he implicitly challenged the traditional view of art as the bearer of noble themes.

Manet further defied tradition by employing new painting techniques. Imitating current photographic practice, he bathed his figures in bright light, flattening them so that they resembled the figures in Japanese prints (figure 31.9). Even Manet's friends were critical: Courbet mockingly compared *Olympia* to the Queen of Spades in a deck of playing cards. Manet's practice of eliminating halftones and laying on fresh, opaque colors (instead of building up form by means of thin, transparent glazes) anticipated impressionism, a style he embraced later in his career.

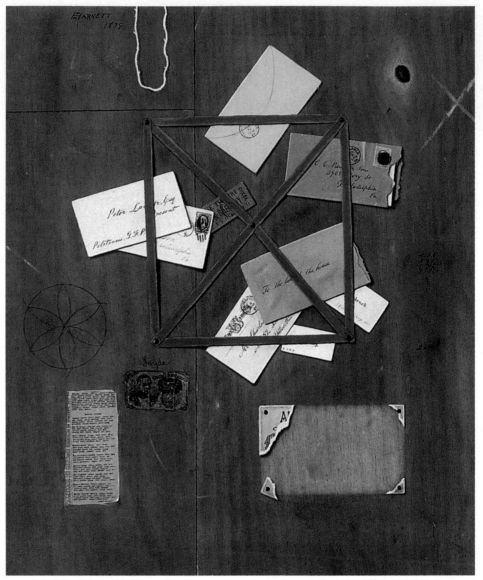

FIGURE 30.16 *The Artist's Letter Rack,* **William Michael Harnett, 1879. Oil on canvas, 30 in. × 25 in. Signed and dated (upper left): WMH (monogram) ARNETT/1879. The Metropolitan Museum of Art, New York City, Morris K. Jesup Fund, 1966. 66.13**

Realism in American Painting

Although most American artists received their training in European art schools, their taste for realism seems to have sprung from a native affection for the factual and the material aspects of their immediate surroundings. In the late nineteenth century, an era of gross materialism known as the Gilded Age, America produced an extraordinary number of first-rate realist painters. These individuals explored a wide variety of subjects, from still life and portraiture to landscape and genre painting. Like such literary giants as Mark Twain, American realist painters fused keen observation with remarkable descriptive skills. One of the most talented of the American realists was William M. Harnett (d. 1892), a still-life painter and a master of *trompe l'oeil* ("fool the eye") illusionism. Working in the tradition of the Dutch still-life masters (figures 22.3 and 22.4), Harnett recorded mundane objects with such hair-fine precision that some of them—letters, newspaper clippings, and calling cards—seem to be pasted on the canvas (figure 30.16).

FIGURE 30.17 *The Agnew Clinic*, Thomas Eakins, 1889. Oil on canvas, 6 ft. 2 1/2 in. × 10 ft. 10 1/2 in. University of Pennsylvania School of Medicine.

In the genre of portraiture, the Philadelphia artist Thomas Eakins (d. 1916) produced uncompromising likenesses such as that of the poet Walt Whitman (figure 27.3). Eakins also painted contemporary activities and occupations, such as boxing, boating, and medical training. *The Agnew Clinic* is a dispassionate view of a hospital amphitheater in which a doctor lectures to students on the subject of a surgical procedure (figure 30.17). Eakins, a photographer of some note, often used the camera to collect visual data for his compositions. He never romanticized his subjects, and while such a painting as *The Agnew Clinic* owes much to Rembrandt's *Anatomy Lesson* (figure 22.14), it represents a fresh and stubbornly precise approach to nature.

If American realists were keenly aware of the new art of photography, they were also indebted to the world of journalism. Winslow Homer (d. 1910) was a newspaper illustrator and a reporter for the New York magazine *Harper's Weekly.* The first professional artist to serve as a war correspondant, Homer produced

paintings and drawings of the American Civil War, which *Harper's* converted to wood-engraved illustrations (figure 30.18). Although Homer often generalized the facts of the events he actually witnessed, he never moralized on his subjects (as did, for instance, Goya or Delacroix). His talent for graphic selectivity and concentration rivaled that of America's first war photographer, Mathew B. Brady (figure 30.4).

Apart from two trips to Europe, Homer spent most of his life in New England, where he painted subjects that were both ordinary and typically American. Scenes of hunting and fishing reveal Homer's deep affection for nature, while his many genre paintings reflect a fascination with the activities of American children. In *The Country School,* Homer used crisply articulated details and stark patterns of light and shadow to convey the controlled atmosphere of rural American education (figure 30.19). Homer was also interested in the activities of black people in contemporary culture. One of his most enigmatic paintings,

FIGURE 30.18 *The War for the Union, 1862—A Bayonet Charge,* Winslow Homer, published in *Harper's Weekly,* July 12, 1862. Wood engraving, 13 5/8 in. × 20 5/8 in. The Metropolitan Museum of Art, New York City, Harris Brisbane Fund, 1929. 29.88.3 (3)

FIGURE 30.19 *The Country School,* Winslow Homer, 1871. Oil on canvas, 21 3/8 in. × 28 3/8 in. St. Louis Art Museum, Museum Purchase.

FIGURE 30.20 *The Gulf Stream,* Winslow Homer, 1899. Oil on canvas, 28 1/8 in. × 49 1/8 in. Signed and dated lower left Homer/1899. The Metropolitan Museum of Art, New York City, Catharine Lorillard Wolfe Collection 1906. 06.1234

The Gulf Stream, shows a black man adrift in a rudderless boat surrounded by shark-filled waters that are whipped by the winds of an impending tornado (figure 30.20). While realistic in execution, the painting may be interpreted as a romantic metaphor for the isolation and plight of modern Blacks. However, compared with the more theatrical rendering of man against nature represented in Géricault's *Raft of the Medusa* (figure 29.13), Homer's painting is a matter-of-fact study of human resignation in the face of deadly peril.

American audiences loved their realist painters, but occasionally, critics voiced mixed feelings. The American novelist Henry James (d. 1916) assessed what he called Homer's "perfect realism," with these words:

> He is almost barbarously simple, and, to our eye, he is horribly ugly; but there is nevertheless something one likes about him. What is it? For ourselves, it is not his subjects. We frankly confess that we detest his subjects— his barren plank fences, his glaring, bald, blue skies, his big, dreary, vacant lots of meadows, his freckled, straight-haired Yankee urchins, his flat-breasted maidens, suggestive of a dish of rural doughnuts and pie, his calico sun-bonnets,

his flannel shirts, his cowhide boots. He has chosen the least pictorial features of the least pictorial range of scenery and civilization; he has resolutely treated them as if they *were* pictorial, as if they were every inch as good as Capri or Tangiers; and, to reward his audacity, he has incontestably succeeded. It . . . is a proof that if you will only be doggedly literal, though you may often be unpleasing, you will at least have a stamp of your own.[4]

Realism in Music

In Italian opera of the late nineteenth century, a movement called **verismo** (literally "truth-ism," but more generally "realism" or "naturalism") paralleled the emphasis on reality in literature and art. Realistic composers rejected the heroic characters of romantic grand opera and portrayed people in familiar and ordinary—if occasionally somewhat melodramatic— situations. The foremost "verist" in music was the Italian composer Giacomo Puccini (d. 1924). Puccini's *La Bohème,* the tragic love story of young artists

---

[4] Quoted in John W. McCoubrey, *American Art 1700–1960. Sources and Documents* (Englewood Cliffs, N.J.: Prentice-Hall, 1965), 165.

(called "bohemians" for their unconventional life-styles) in the Latin Quarter of Paris, was based on a nineteenth-century novel called *Scenes of Bohemian Life*. The colorful orchestration and powerfully melodic arias of *La Bohème* evoke the joys and sorrows of true-to-life characters. While this poignant musical drama was received coldly at its premiere in 1897, *La Bohème* has become one of the best-loved of nineteenth-century grand operas.

Summary

During the second half of the nineteenth century, as the social consequences of Western industrialism became increasingly visible, realism came to rival romanticism both as a style and as an attitude of mind. The nineteenth-century ideologies of liberalism, conservatism, utilitarianism, socialism, and communism offered varying solutions to contemporary problems of social injustice and inequality. In *The Communist Manifesto,* Marx and Engels called for the violent revolution of the proletariat and the abolition of private ownership of the means of economic production. The leading proponent of liberalism, John Stuart Mill, defended the exercise of individual liberty as protected by the state. Mill's opposition to the subjection of women gave strong support to nineteenth-century movements for women's rights.

In the arts, realism emerged as a style concerned with recording contemporary subject matter in true-to-life terms. Such novelists as Charles Dickens in England, Dostoevsky and Tolstoy in Russia, Flaubert and Zola in France, and Mark Twain in America described contemporary social conditions sympathetically and with fidelity to detail. Flaubert provided an alternative to romantic idealism in the realistic characterization of Emma Bovary. Zola's novels introduced a naturalistic perception of human beings as determined by hereditary and sociological factors. Ibsen pioneered modern drama in his fearless portrayal of class and gender conflicts.

Photography and lithography were invented during the nineteenth century; both media encouraged artists to produce objective records of their surroundings. By the mid-nineteenth century the camera was used to document all aspects of contemporary life as well as to provide artists with detailed visual data for their paintings. In painting, Courbet led the realist movement with canvases depicting the activities of humble and commonplace men and women. Daumier employed the new technique of lithography to show his deep concern for political and social conditions in rapidly modernizing France. Manet shocked art critics by recasting traditional subjects in contemporary terms. America's realist painters, including Thomas Eakins and Winslow Homer, recorded typically American pastimes in an unembellished, forthright manner. Though realism did not adapt itself to music in any specific manner, the Italian "verist" Puccini wrote operas that captured the lives of nineteenth-century Europeans with a truth to nature reminiscent of realist novels and paintings. On the whole, the varieties of realism in nineteenth-century cultural expression reflect a profound concern for social and economic inequities and offer a critical reassessment of traditional Western values.

GLOSSARY

capitalist one who provides investment capital in economic ventures

entrepreneur one who organizes, manages, and assumes the risks of a business

proletariat a collective term describing industrial workers who lack their own means of production and hence sell their labor to live

lithography a printmaking process created by drawing on a stone plate; see figure 30.9

verismo (Italian, "realism") a type of late nineteenth-century opera that presents a realistic picture of life, instead of a story based in myth, legend, or ancient history

SUGGESTIONS FOR READING

Barzun, Jacques. *Darwin, Marx, and Wagner.* 2d ed. New York: Columbia University Press, 1981.

Baumer, Franklin L., ed. *Intellectual Movements in Modern European History.* London: Macmillan, 1965.

Berlin, Isaiah. *Karl Marx: His Life and Environment.* New York: Oxford University Press, 1978.

Clark, T. J. *The Painting of Modern Life: Paris in the Art of Manet and His Followers.* New York: Knopf, 1984.

Duncan, Graeme C. *Marx and Mill: Two Views of Social Conflict and Social Harmony.* Cambridge: Cambridge University Press, 1973.

Hamilton, G. H. *Manet and His Critics.* New Haven, Conn.: Yale University Press, 1986.

Larkin, Maurice. *Man and Society in Nineteenth-Century Realism, Determinism and Literature.* Totowa, N.J.: Rowman and Littlefield, 1977.

Nochlin, Linda. *Realism.* New York: Penguin, 1971.

Schneider, Pierre. *The World of Manet, 1832–1883.* Library of Art. New York: Time-Life Books, 1968.

Smart, Paul. *Mill and Marx: Individual Liberty and the Roads to Freedom.* New York: St. Martin's, 1991.

Stromberg, Roland N., ed. *Realism, Naturalism and Symbolism: Modes of Thought and Expression in Europe, 1848–1914.* New York: Walker, 1968.

Struik, Dirk J., ed. *The Birth of the Communist Manifesto.* New York: International Publishers, 1971.

31

ART FOR ART'S SAKE

During the last quarter of the nineteenth century, France was the center of most of the important developments in the arts of Western Europe. Especially in Paris, poets, painters, and composers turned their backs on both romanticism and realism. They pursued styles that neither idealized the world nor described it with reforming zeal. Their art was more concerned with sensory experience than with moral purpose, with feeling than with teaching. Unlike their predecessors, these artists did not create in order to exalt the true, the noble, or the sacred; rather, they made art for art's sake.

Late nineteenth-century science and technology helped to shape this new approach in the arts. In 1873, the British physicist James Clerk Maxwell (d. 1879) published his *Treatise on Electricity and Magnetism,* which explained that light waves consisting of electromagnetic particles produced radiant energy. In 1879, after numerous failures, the American inventor Thomas Edison (d. 1931) moved beyond scientific theory to create the first efficient incandescent light bulb. Incandescent electric light provided a sharper perception of reality that—along with the camera—helped to shatter the world of romantic illusion. By the year 1880, the telephone transported the human voice over thousands of miles. In the late 1880s Edison developed the technique of moving pictures. And, in 1897, the invention of the internal combustion engine made possible the first automobiles. Such developments accelerated the tempo of life and drew attention to the role of the senses in defining experience.

As is often the case in the history of culture, late nineteenth-century philosophic theory mirrored other forms of contemporary expression. Henri Bergson (d. 1941), the most important French philosopher of his day, provided a view of reality that not only paralleled key developments in the arts and sciences but anticipated modern notions of time and space. Bergson viewed life as a vital impulse that evolved creatively, much like a work of art. According to Bergson, two primary powers, intellect and intuition, governed the lives of human beings. While intellect perceives experience in individual and discrete terms, or as a series of separate and solid entities, intuition grasps experience as it really is: a perpetual stream of sensations. Intellect isolates and categorizes experience according to logic and geometry; intuition, on the other hand, fuses past and present into one organic whole. For Bergson, instinct, or intuition, is humankind's noblest faculty, and *duration,* or "perpetual becoming," is the very stuff of reality— the essence of life. In 1889, Bergson published his treatise *Time and Freewill,* in which he explained that true experience is durational, a constant unfolding in time, and that reality, which can only be apprehended intuitively, is a series of qualitative changes that merge into one another without precise outlines.

Poetry in the Late Nineteenth Century: The Symbolists

Bergson's poetical view of nature had much in common with the aesthetics of many late nineteenth-century artists, including that of the *symbolists*. The symbolists, who included the French poets Paul Verlaine (d. 1896), Arthur Rimbaud (d. 1891), and Stéphane Mallarmé (d. 1898), and the Belgian playwright Maurice Maeterlinck (d. 1949), tried to capture in language the ineffable dimension of intuitive experience. They rejected both the romanticism and the realism/naturalism of nineteenth-century writers and tried to free language from its traditional descriptive and expressive functions. They wrote verse that evoked the fleeting and incommunicable nature of experience. For such poets, reality was a swarm of sensations that could never be described but only translated via poetic symbols—verbal images that, through the power of suggestion, elicited moods and feelings beyond the literal meanings of words. In one of the prose poems from his *Illuminations,* for example, Rimbaud described flowers as "Bits of yellow gold seeded in agate, pillars of mahogany supporting a dome of emeralds, bouquets of white satin and fine rods of ruby surround the water rose."[1] The symbolists tried to represent nature without effusive commentary, to "take eloquence and wring its neck," as Verlaine put it. In order to imitate the indefiniteness of experience itself, they might string images together without logical connections. Hence, in symbolist poetry, images seem to flow into one another, and "meaning" often lies between the lines.

For Stéphane Mallarmé, the "new art" of poetry was a religion, and the poet-artist was its oracle. Unlike realist writers, who stressed social interaction and reform, Mallarmé withdrew from the world; he held that art was "accessible only to the few" who nurtured "the inner life." Mallarmé's poems are tapestries of sensuous, dreamlike motifs that resist definition and analysis. To name a thing, Mallarmé insisted, was to destroy it, while to suggest experience was to create it. Such were the principles that inspired Mallarmé's pastoral poem, *"L'Après-midi d'un faune"* ("Afternoon of a Faun"). The poem is a reverie of an erotic encounter between two mythological woodland creatures, a faun (part man, part beast) and a nymph (a beautiful forest maiden). As the faun awakens, he tries to recapture the experiences of the previous afternoon. Whether his elusive memories belong to the world of dreams or to reality is uncertain; but, true to Bergson's theory of duration, reality becomes a stream of sensations in which past and present merge. As the following excerpt illustrates, Mallarmé's rhythms are free and hypnotic, and his images, which follow one another with few logical transitions, are intimately linked to the world of the senses.

READING 109   From Mallarmé's "Afternoon of a Faun"

I would immortalize these nymphs: so bright
Their sunlit coloring, so airy light,
It floats like drowsing down. Loved I a dream?
My doubts, born of oblivious darkness, seem
A subtle tracery of branches grown
The tree's true self—proving that I have known,
Thinking it love, the blushing of a rose.
But think. These nymphs, their loveliness . . . suppose
They bodied forth your senses' fabulous thirst?
Illusion! which the blue eyes of the first,   10
As cold and chaste as is the weeping spring,
Beget: the other, sighing, passioning,
Is she the wind, warm in your fleece at noon?
No; through this quiet, when a weary swoon
Crushes and chokes the latest faint essay
Of morning, cool against the encroaching day,
There is no murmuring water, save the gush
Of my clear fluted notes; and in the hush
Blows never a wind, save that which through my reed[2]
Puffs out before the rain of notes can speed   20
Upon the air, with that calm breath of art
That mounts the unwrinkled zenith visibly,
Where inspiration seeks its native sky.
You fringes of a calm Sicilian lake,
The sun's own mirror which I love to take,
Silent beneath your starry flowers, tell
How here I cut the hollow rushes, well
Tamed by my skill, when on the glaucous gold
Of distant lawns about their fountain cold
A living whiteness stirs like a lazy wave;   30
And at the first slow notes my panpipes gave
These flocking swans, these naiads, rather, fly
Or dive.

.   .   .   .

See how the ripe pomegranates bursting red
To quench the thirst of the mumbling bees have bled;
So too our blood, kindled by some chance fire,
Flows for the swarming legions of desire.
At evening, when the woodland green turns gold

---

[1] *The Norton Anthology of World Literature,* 4th ed. (New York: W. W. Norton, 1980), 1188.

[2] A pipe or flute.

And ashen grey, 'mid the quenched leaves, behold!
Red Etna[3] glows, by Venus visited,   40
Walking the lava with her snowy tread
Whene'er the flames in thunderous slumber die.
I hold the goddess!

                    Ah, sure penalty!

But the unthinking soul and body swoon
At last beneath the heavy hush of noon.
Forgetful let me lie where summer's drouth
Sifts fine the sand and then with gaping mouth
Dream planet-struck by the grape's round wine-red star.

Nymphs, I shall see the shade that now you are.   50

---

[3]A volcanic mountain in Sicily.

Music in the Late Nineteenth Century: Debussy

It is no surprise that symbolist poetry, itself a form of music, found its counterpart in music. Like the poetry of Mallarmé, the music of Claude Debussy (d. 1918) engages the listener through nuance and atmosphere. Debussy's compositions consist of broken fragments of melody, the outlines of which are blurred and indistinct. "I would like to see the creation . . . of a kind of music without themes and motives," wrote Debussy, "formed on a single continuous theme, which is uninterrupted and which never returns on itself."

Debussy owed much to Richard Wagner and the romantic composers who had abandoned the formal clarity of classical composition (chapter 29). He was also indebted to the exotic music of Bali and Indonesia, which he had heard performed at the Paris Exposition of 1889. Debussy experimented with the five-tone scale found in East Asian music and with nontraditional kinds of harmony. He deviated from the traditional Western practice of returning harmonies to the tonic, or "home tone," introducing instead shifting harmonies with no clearly defined tonal center. His rich harmonic palette, characterized by unusually constructed chords, reflects a fascination with tone color that may have been inspired by the writings of the German physiologist Hermann van Helmholtz (d. 1884)—especially Helmholtz's treatise *On the Sensations of Tone as a Physiological Basis for the Theory of Music* (1863). But Debussy found his greatest source of inspiration in contemporary poetry and painting. Debussy was a close friend of many of the symbolist poets, whose texts he often set to music. His first orchestral composition, *Prelude to "The Afternoon of a Faun"* (1894),$^{\flat}$ was (in his words) a "very free illustration of a Mallarmé's beautiful poem," which had been published eighteen years earlier. Debussy originally intended to write a dramatic piece based on the poem, but he ultimately produced a ten-minute orchestral prelude that shares the dreamlike quality of the poem. (In 1912, Debussy's score became the basis for a twelve-minute ballet choreographed by the Russian dancer Nijinsky; see chapter 32.)

Debussy had little use for the ponderous orchestras of the German romantics. He scored the *Prelude* for a small orchestra whose unusual combination of wind and brass instruments might recreate Mallarmé's delicate mood of reverie. A sensuous melody for unaccompanied flute provides the composition's opening theme, which is then developed by flutes, oboes, and clarinets. Harp, triangle, muted horns, and lightly brushed cymbals contribute luminous tonal textures that—like the images of the poem itself—seem based in pure sensation. Transitions are subtle rather than focused, and melodies seem to drift without resolution. Imprecise tone clusters and shifting harmonies create misty, nebulous effects that call to mind the shimmering effects of light on water and the ebb and flow of ocean waves. Indeed, water, a favorite motif of impressionist art, is the subject of many of Debussy's works, such as *Gardens in the Rain* (1903), *Image: Reflections in the Water* (1905), and *The Sea* (1905).

Painting in the Late Nineteenth Century: Impressionism

What the symbolists sought in poetry, and Debussy pursued in music, the French *impressionists* achieved in paint. Luminosity, the interaction of light and form, subtlety of tone, and a preoccupation with sensation itself were the major features of impressionist art. Impressionist subject matter preserved the romantic fascination with nature and the realist preoccupation with the late nineteen-century French society. But impressionism differed from both romanticism, which generally idealized nature, and realism, which tried to record nature with unbiased objectivity. An art of pure sensation, impressionism was, in part, a response to nineteenth-century research in the physics of light, the chemistry of paint, and the laws of optics.

FIGURE 31.1 *Impression: Sunrise,* Claude Monet, 1873. Oil on canvas, 19 5/8 in. × 25 1/2 in. Musée Marmottan, Paris. Scala/Art Resource, New York.

Such publications as *Principles of Harmony and the Contrast of Colors* by the French chemist Michel Chevreul (d. 1889), along with treatises on the physical properties of color and musical tone by Hermann von Helmholtz offered new insights into the psychology of perception. At the same time, late nineteenth-century chemists produced the first synthetic pigments, which replaced traditional earth pigments with brilliant new colors. Such developments in science and technology contributed to the birth of the new art of light and color.

Monet: Pioneer of Impressionism

In 1872 the French artist Claude Monet exhibited a work of art that some critics consider the first modern painting. *Impression: Sunrise* is patently a seascape; but the painting says more about *how* one sees than about *what* one sees (figure 31.1). It transcribes the fleeting effects of light and the changing atmosphere of water and air into a tissue of small dots and streaks of color—the elements of pure perception. To achieve luminosity, Monet coated the raw canvas with gesso, a chalklike medium. Then, working in the open air and using the new chemical paints (available in the form of portable metallic tubes), he rapidly applied brushstrokes of pure, occasionally unmixed color. Monet ignored the brown underglazes artists traditionally used to build up form. And, arguing that there were no "lines" in nature, he refused to delineate forms with fixed contours; rather, he evoked form with color. Instead of blending his colors to create a finished effect, he placed them side by side, building up a radiant impasto. In order to intensify visual effect, he juxtaposed complementary colors, putting touches of orange (red and yellow) next to blue and adding bright tints of rose, pink, and vermillion (figure 31.2).

FIGURE 31.2 Detail of figure 31.1

In place of black, Monet created shadows out of colors complementary to the hue of the object casting the shadows, thus more closely approximating the prismatic effects of light on the human eye. The result was a painting that recorded the instantaneous visual sensations of light itself.

Monet was by no means the first painter to deviate from academic techniques. Constable had applied color in rough dots and dabs, Delacroix occasionally had juxtaposed complementary colors to increase brilliance, and Manet had often omitted halftones in the definition of form. But Monet went further by interpreting form as color itself. Consequently, *Impression: Sunrise* struck the critics as a radically new approach in art. One critic dismissed the painting as "only an impression," no better than "wallpaper in its embryonic state," thus, unwittingly giving the name "impressionism" to the movement that would dominate French art of the 1870s and 1880s.

FIGURE 31.3 *Rouen Cathedral, West Facade Sunlight,* Claude Monet, 1894. Oil on canvas, 39 1/2 in. × 26 in. National Gallery of Art, Chester Dale Collection, 1962.

The subjects of Monet's early works included street scenes, picnics, café life, and boating parties at the fashionable tourist resorts that dotted the banks of the Seine River near Paris. However, as Monet found light and color more compelling than Parisian society, his paintings became more impersonal and formless. Wishing, as he put it, to "seize the intangible," he painted the changing effects of light on such mundane objects as poplar trees and haystacks. Often

working on a number of canvases at once, he might generate a series of paintings that showed his subject in morning light, under the noon sun, at sunset, and so on. Between 1892 and 1894, after a trip to England during which he became familiar with the colorist landscapes of Turner (figures 29.3 and 29.4), Monet produced twenty different versions of the west facade of Rouen Cathedral (figure 31.3). For Monet, this great monument of medieval Christendom might just as

FIGURE 31.4 *Le Moulin de la Galette,* **Pierre Auguste Renoir, 1876. Oil on canvas, 51 1/2 in. × 69 in. Scala/Art Resource, New York.**

well have been a haystack or a pond of water lilies—the favorite subject of his late life at Giverny, his summer home some forty miles from Paris. Indeed, Monet seized the cathedral, as he did these other subjects, with his eye rather than with his intellect, and he rendered it not as a sacred symbol but as a physical sensation.

Monet may be considered an ultrarealist in his effort to reproduce with absolute fidelity the ever-changing effects of light on the human eye. His freedom from preconceived ideas of nature prompted his contemporary Paul Cézanne to exclaim that he was "only an eye, but," he added admiringly, "what an eye!" Ironically, Monet's devotion to the physical truth of nature paved the way for modern abstraction—the concern with the intrinsic qualities of the subject, rather than with its literal appearance.

Renoir, Degas, and Cassatt

Impressionism was never a single, uniform style; rather, the designation embraced the individual approaches of many different artists throughout Europe and America. Nevertheless, the group of artists who met regularly in the 1870s and 1880s at the Café Guerbois in Paris had much in common. Like most of the impressionists, Pierre Auguste Renoir (d. 1919) recorded the intimate pleasures of daily life—dining, bathing, music making, and dancing. Le Moulin de la Galette, an outdoor café and dancehall located in Montmartre (the bohemian section of nineteenth-century Paris), provided the setting for one of Renoir's most ravishing tributes to youth and pleasure (figure 31.4). In the painting, elegantly dressed young men and women—artists, students, and lower-middle-class members of Parisian society—dance, drink, and

FIGURE 31.5 *The False Start,* Edgar Degas, ca. 1870. Oil on canvas, 12 5/8 in. × 15 3/4 in. Yale University Art Gallery, John Hay Whitney, B.A., 1926 Collection.

flirt with one another in the flickering golden light of the late afternoon sun. Renoir's friends and contemporaries, Alfred Sisley (d. 1899), Camille Pisarro (d. 1903), and Berthe Morisot (d. 1895), produced similarly engaging impressions of a society that enjoyed fresh air, good times, and increasing amounts of leisure and affluence.

Edgar Degas (d. 1917) regularly exhibited with the impressionists; but his style remained unique, for Degas never sacrificed line and form to the beguiling qualities of color and light. Whether depicting the urban world of cafés, racecourses, theaters, and shops, or the demimonde of laundresses and prostitutes, Degas concentrated his attention on the fleeting and intimate event (figure 31.5). He rejected the traditional "posed" model as a subject, seeking instead to capture momentary and even awkward gestures such as stretching and yawning. Degas' untiring attention

to racehorses and ballet dancers mirrored his lifelong fascination with matters of balance and motion (figure 31.6). In his efforts to re-create the appearance of physical movement in space, he learned much from the British artist Eadweard Muybridge (d. 1904), whose stop-action photographs of the 1870s and 1880s were revolutionary in their time (figure 31.7).

Degas was a consummate draftsman and a master designer. He used innovative compositional techniques that imparted a sense of spontaneity and improvisation. For instance, he might represent objects as if seen from above or below (figure 31.6). He also experimented with asymmetrical compositions in which figures and objects (or fragments of either) might appear at the edge of the canvas, as if the image were caught at random. Such innovations testify to the influence of photography, with its accidental "slice of life" potential, as well as that of Japanese woodcuts.

FIGURE 31.6 *Before the Ballet*, Edgar Degas, 1888. Oil on canvas, 15 3/4 in. × 35 in. National Gallery of Art, Washington, Widener Collection.

FIGURE 31.7 *Photo Sequence of Racehorse*, Eadweard Muybridge, 1884–85. Photograph. Library of Congress, Washington, D.C.

FIGURE 31.8 *The River Bridge at Uji*, Japanese, Momoyama period, 1568–1614. Ink, colors and gold on paper, 67 1/2 in. × 133 1/4 in. The Nelson-Atkins Museum of Art, Kansas City, Missouri, (Nelson Fund 58–53 1,2).

Japanese prints entered Europe along with other Asian goods in the 1860s. Though they were a new commodity for European collectors and artists, they represented the end of a long tradition of Japanese decorative design. This tradition, which looked back to the secular art of the Heian period (A.D. 794—1185), ultimately flowered in the magnificent folding screens of the sixteenth through eighteenth centuries. Usually executed on a ground of gold leaf, the landscapes that were the favorite subjects of Japanese artists featured flat, bold colors, undulating lines, and unusual perspectives—for instance, bird's eye or worm's eye views (figure 31.8). Similar features characterized popular Japanese prints of the eighteenth and nineteenth centuries, whose subject matter came from everyday life, especially from the world of theater and dance (figure 31.9). Thousands of prints showing famous actors, popular courtesans, and views of noted tourist landmarks found their way to Europe, often in the form of wrapping paper for Japanese imports. The French art critic and enthusiast of impressionist painting, Théodore Duret (d. 1927), was one of the first writers to observe the impact of Japanese prints on nineteenth-century artists. In a pamphlet called *The Impressionist Painters* (1878), Duret explained,

FIGURE 31.9 *Actor as a Monkey Showman*, Torii Kiyonobu, n.d. Woodblock print, 13 1/4 in. × 6 1/4 in. Metropolitan Museum of Art, New York City, Rogers Fund, 1936. JP 2623

We had to wait until the arrival of Japanese albums before anyone dared to sit down on the bank of a river to juxtapose on canvas a boldly red roof, a white wall, a green poplar, a yellow road, and blue water. Before Japan it was impossible; the painter always lied. Nature with its frank colors was in plain sight, yet no one ever saw anything on canvas but attenuated colors, drowning in a general halftone.

As soon as people looked at Japanese pictures, where the most glaring, piercing colors were placed side by side, they finally understood that there were new methods for reproducing certain effects of nature.[4]

Among the many artists influenced by Japanese prints was the American painter Mary Cassatt (d. 1926). Cassatt was born in Pennsylvania but spent most of her life in Paris, where she became a friend and colleague of Degas, Morisot, and Renoir and the impressionists, with whom she exhibited regularly. Like Degas, she painted mainly indoors, cultivating a style that combined forceful calligraphy, large areas of unmodulated color, and unusual perspectives—the major features of the Japanese woodcuts. Cassatt brought a unique sensitivity to domestic subjects, such as scenes of mothers and children enjoying everyday tasks and pleasures (figure 31.10). These gentle and optimistic images appealed to American collectors and did much to increase the popularity of impressionist art in the United States.

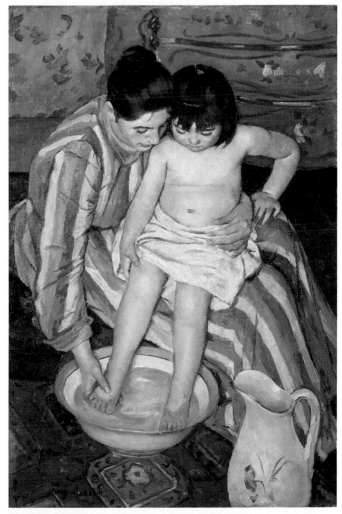

FIGURE 31.10 *The Bath*, Mary Cassatt, 1891–92. Oil on canvas, 39 1/2 in. × 26 in. Robert A. Waller Fund, 1910–12, photograph © 1991, The Art Institute of Chicago. All rights reserved.

[4]Quoted in Linda Nochlin, *Impressionism and Post-Impressionism 1874–1904* (Englewood Cliffs, N.J.: Prentice-Hall, 1966), 8–9.

FIGURE 31.11 *At the Moulin-Rouge,* Henri de Toulouse-Lautrec, 1892. Oil on canvas, 48 3/8 in. × 55 1/4 in. Helen Birch Bartlett Memorial Collection, 1928. 610, photograph © 1991, The Art Institute of Chicago. All rights reserved.

FIGURE 31.12 *Jane Avril,* Henri de Toulouse-Lautrec, 1899. Lithographic poster, printed in color, composition: 22 1/16 in. × 11 3/4 in. Collection, The Museum of Modern Art, New York. Gift of Abby Aldrich Rockefeller.

The Cabaret World of Toulouse-Lautrec

While the paintings of Renoir and Cassatt seem filled with sunshine and fresh air, those of the French artist Henri de Toulouse-Lautrec (d. 1901) reek of stale cigars and beer (figure 31.11). Toulouse-Lautrec left an indelible record of the seamy side of Parisian life—the life of cabaret dancers and prostitutes who, like Zola's Nana, lived on the margins of middle-class society. Toulouse-Lautrec self-consciously mocked traditional ideas of beauty and propriety. He stylized figures—almost to the point of caricature—in bold and forceful silhouettes. Fleshtones might be distorted by artificial light or altered by the stark, white makeup (borrowed from Japanese theater) that was in current fashion. Toulouse-Lautrec pioneered the art of poster design. His color lithographs, with their bright, flat colors, their sinuous lines, and their startling juxtapositions of positive and negative space (figure 31.12), reflect his indebtedness to popular Japanese prints (figure 31.9), even as they advertise the voluptuous pleasures of Parisian nightlife.

FIGURE 31.13 Tassel House, Brussels, Victor Horta, 1892–93. Photo: © Bastin & Evrard Photodesigners.

Art Nouveau

The posters of Toulouse-Lautrec bear the seductive stamp of *art nouveau* (French for "new art")—an ornamental style that became enormously popular in the late nineteenth century. Art nouveau artists, who sought a return to the fine artisanship of the Middle Ages, favored bold, flat, organic patterns and semi-abstract linear designs. Art nouveau originated in Belgium among architects working in the medium of cast iron, but it soon became an international movement that influenced painting, as well as the design of furniture, textiles, jewelry, and glass and ceramic wares. The Belgian founder of art nouveau, Victor Horta (d. 1947), typified the art for art's sake spirit. A distinguished architect and a great admirer of Eiffel's thousand-foot-high tower (figure 29.20), Horta translated the serpentine lines and organic rhythms of flowers and plants into metalwork designs for public buildings and private residences (figure 31.13). The sinuous curves of blossoms, leaves, and tendrils, conceived in iron and immortalized in such notable monuments as the Paris Métro (the subway), also showed up in wallpaper, poster design, and book illustration.

In America, the style briefly attracted the attention of such architects as Louis Sullivan, who embellished parts of his otherwise austere office buildings and department stores with floral cast iron ornamentation. It also inspired the magnificent glass designs of Louis Comfort Tiffany (figure 31.14).

Sculpture in the Late Nineteenth Century: Degas and Rodin

While art nouveau artists brought a new organic naturalism to decorative design, the two greatest sculptors of the late nineteenth century, Edgar Degas and Auguste Rodin (d. 1917), tried to capture the organic vitality of figural movement and gesture. Like the impressionists, Degas and Rodin were interested in re-creating the sensory effects of light. In order to catch these fleeting qualities, they modeled their figures rapidly in wet clay. The bronze casts made from these clay originals preserve the spontaneity of this additive process.

FIGURE 31.14 Peacock vase, Tiffany Glass and Decorating Co., 1892–1902, Corona, New York. Iridescent "favrile" glass, blues and greens with feather and eye decorations, height, 14 1/8 in. × 11 1/2 in. The Metropolitan Museum of Art. Gift of H. O. Havemeyer, 1896. 96.17.10

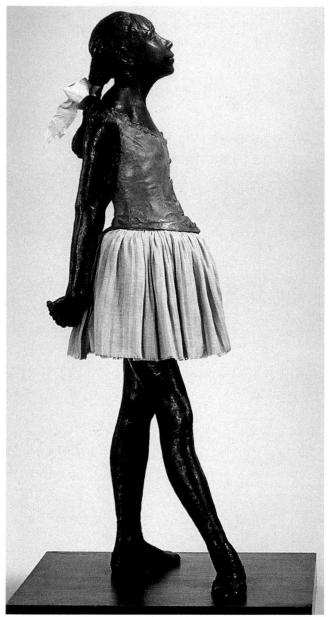

FIGURE 31.15 *Little Fourteen-Year-Old Dancer,* Edgar Degas, 1880–81. Probably cast in bronze, tulle skirt and satin hair ribbon, height 39 in. The Metropolitan Museum of Art, New York City. Bequest of Mrs. H. O. Havemeyer, 1929. The H.O. Havemeyer Collection. 29.100.370 View #2

FIGURE 31.16 *Dancing Figure,* Auguste Rodin, 1905. Graphite with orange wash, 12 3/4 in. × 9 1/2 in. National Gallery of Art, Washington, gift of Mrs. John W. Simpson.

Degas' engaging bronze *Little Fourteen-Year-Old Dancer* retains the fluid grace of his finest drawings and paintings (figure 31.15). The surfaces of the figure tend to dissolve in light, while the gauze tutu and satin bow—the addition of which anticipated the multimedia innovations of twentieth-century artists—provide sensuous textural contrasts to the solid form. Especially in the years when Degas' vision began to decline, he turned to modeling clay "sketches" of race horses, bathers, and ballerinas—his favorite subjects. These miniature masterpieces still bear the imprints of his fingers and fingernails.

Like Degas, Rodin was deeply interested in movement and gesture. In hundreds of drawings, he recorded the dancelike rhythms of studio models whom he bid to move about freely rather than assume traditional, fixed poses (figure 31.16). But it was in the three-dimensional media that Rodin made his greatest contribution. One of his earliest sculptures, *The Age of Bronze,* was so lifelike that critics accused him of forging the figure from plaster casts of a live model (figure 31.17). In actuality, Rodin had captured a sense of organic movement by recreating the fleeting effects of light on form. Here, as in his later works, he heightened the contrasts between polished and roughly textured surfaces, deliberately leaving parts of the piece unfinished. "Sculpture," declared Rodin, "is quite simply the art of depression and protuberance."

But Rodin moved beyond naturalistic representation to wring from volume (as the symbolists wrung from language) specific states of feeling. He gave his

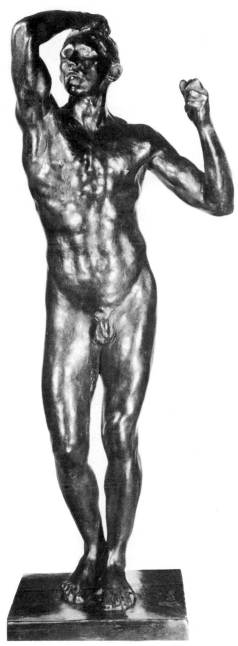

FIGURE 31.17 *The Age of Bronze,* Auguste Rodin, 1876. Bronze, 25 1/2 in. × 9 5/16 in. × 7 1/2 in. © Detroit Institute of Arts, gift of Robert H. Tannahill. 69.304

FIGURE 31.18 Isadora Duncan in *La Marseillaise.* Collection of the Library of Congress, Washington, D.C.

figures a nervous energy and an emotional intensity that was lacking in both classical and renaissance sculpture. "The sculpture of antiquity," he explained, "sought the logic of the human body; I seek its psychology." In this quest, Rodin was joined by his close friend, the American dancer Isadora Duncan (d. 1927). Duncan, who rebelled against the rules of classical ballet by dancing with bare feet, introduced a new style of dance based on free-form, personalized

gestures and movements (figure 31.18). Both Duncan and Rodin investigated the ways in which the body's outward form expressed inner states of feeling. As in Duncan's choreography, so in Rodin's greatest pieces, a particular psychological condition often constitutes the subject matter. Such is also the case with the figures that make up Rodin's masterpiece, *The Gates of Hell,* a set of doors designed for the projected Paris

FIGURE 31.19 *The Gates of Hell*, Auguste Rodin, 1880–1917. Bronze, 250 3/4 in. × 158 in. × 33 3/8 in. Rodin Museum, Philadelphia, gift of Jules E. Mastbaum.

Museum of Decorative Arts (figure 31.19). For this aborted commission, Rodin created the figures that he would later recast individually in bronze or (with the help of studio assistants) in marble. The most famous of these individual sculptures are *The Kiss* and *The Thinker*—the latter originally represented Dante contemplating the underworld from atop its portals. Like the symbolist poems of Mallarmé, or the impressionist paintings of Monet, Rodin's "Gates" are a swarm of powerful images assembled without logical transitions. Each image melts into the next and the whole operates through the power of suggestion.

Postimpressionism and the Art for Art's Sake Spirit

The artists who followed the impressionists—the *postimpressionists*—continued to reflect the prevailing spirit of art for art's sake. The postimpressionists were largely disinterested in satisfying the demands of public and private patrons; they made only sporadic efforts to sell what they produced. Although strongly individualistic, they were all profoundly preoccupied with the formal language of art and its capacity to capture sensory experience. Like impressionism, postimpressionism can be seen as an intensification of romantic artists' efforts to share their subjective responses to the real world. But unlike the romantics (and the impressionists), the postimpressionists made a conscious effort to move beyond the world of pure sensation. These pioneers of modern art put into practice the point of view of the French artist and theorist Maurice Denis (d. 1943): Denis believed that a painting was not first and foremost a pictorial reproduction of reality but was essentially "a flat surface covered with shapes, lines, and colors assembled in a particular order." This credo, as realized in postimpressionist painting, inspired most of the major modern art movements of the early twentieth century (chapter 32).

The Postimpressionists van Gogh and Gauguin

The Dutch artist Vincent van Gogh (d. 1890) was a passionate idealist whose life was marred by loneliness, depression, and a hereditary mental illness that ultimately drove him to suicide. During his career as an artist, he produced over seven hundred paintings and thousands of drawings, of which he sold less than a half-dozen in his lifetime. Influenced by Japanese prints, van Gogh painted landscapes, still lifes, and portraits in a style that featured flat, bright colors, a throbbing, sinuous line, and short, choppy brushstrokes. His heavily pigmented surfaces were often manipulated by a palette knife or built up by applying paint directly from the tube.

Van Gogh shared with the romantics an attitude toward nature that was both inspired and ecstatic. His response to the world rather than its physical appearance often determined his choice of colors. As he explained to his brother Theo, "I use color more arbitrarily so as to express myself more forcefully." Van Gogh's painting *The Starry Night* (1889), a landscape that features a view of the small French town of Saint-Rémy, is electrified by thickly painted strokes of white, yellow, orange, and blue (figure 31.20). Cypresses writhe like tongues of flame, stars explode, the moon seems to burn like the sun, and the heavens heave and roll like ocean waves. Here, van Gogh's expressive use of color invests nature with visionary frenzy.

If van Gogh may be said to have apprehended an inner vision of nature, Paul Gauguin (d. 1903) tried to embrace nature in its unblemished state. Abandoning his wife, his children, and his job as a Paris stockbroker, this prototype of the modern bohemian traveled to Martinique, to Brittany (in Northwest France), and to Southern France before finally settling on the island of Tahiti in the South Seas. Gauguin's self-conscious effort to assume the role of "the civilized savage" shared the fascination with unspoiled nature that characterized the writings of Rousseau and Thoreau. And in this sense, Gauguin's bohemianism represented the "last gasp" of romanticism. But Gauguin's flight to the South Seas was also typical of *neoprimitivism,* the fascination with non-Western cultures that swept through the intellectual community of late nineteenth-century Europe. The Paris Exhibition of 1889 brought to public view the native arts of Africa, Asia, and Oceania (the islands of the Central and South Pacific). Remote societies and their achievements were becoming objects of study for the new discipline of anthropology, the science of humankind and its culture. In 1890, the Scottish anthropologist Sir James Frazer (d. 1941) published *The Golden Bough,* a pioneer study of magic and religion as reflected in ancient and tribal folk customs. (Frazer's work would become even more influential when it was reissued in a twelve-volume edition between 1911 and 1915.) The lure of the primitive among such late nineteenth-century figures as Gauguin represented a rebellion against Western sexual and societal taboos—a rebellion that would become fullblown in the neoprimitivism of early modern art (see chapter 32).

FIGURE 31.20 *The Starry Night,* Vincent van Gogh, 1889. Oil on canvas, 29 in. × 36 1/4 in. Collection, The Museum of Modern Art, New York. Acquired through the Lillie P. Bliss Bequest.

FIGURE 31.21 *The Day of the God (Mahana no Atua),* Paul Gauguin, 1894. Oil on canvas, 27 3/8 in. × 35 5/8 in. Helen Birch Bartlett Memorial Collection, 1926.198, photograph © 1991, The Art Institute of Chicago. All Rights Reserved.

Gauguin's painting style likewise constituted a rebellion against Western tradition. It featured brightly colored shapes that seem to float on the surface of the canvas. In *The Day of the God* (1894), bright blues, yellows, and pinks form tapestry-like patterns that have little to do with the appearance of actual objects in space (figure 31.21). Like the images of the symbolist poets, Gauguin's forms and colors suggest or evoke a mood. They do not describe; rather, they *imply* ideas that lie beyond literal description. For example, the organic shapes in the foreground pool of water and the fetal positions of the figures lying on the shore are suggestive of birth and regeneration.

Gauguin's figures cast no shadows, and his bold, unmodeled colors, like those of van Gogh, often bear little relationship to visual appearance. (The blues in the background of *The Day of the God,* for instance, are of the same intensity as those in the foreground.) Gauguin joined van Gogh at Arles in the fall of 1888, and for a brief time the two artists worked together. Volatile and temperamental, they often engaged in violent quarrels, and during one of van Gogh's psychotic episodes (which ended in his cutting off part of his own ear), he even attempted to kill Gauguin. But despite their intense personal differences, van Gogh and Gauguin were fraternal pioneers in the search for a provocative language of color.

FIGURE 31.22 *Sunday Afternoon on the Island of La Grande Jatte,* Georges Seurat, 1884–86. Oil on canvas, 81 in. × 120 3/8 in. Helen Birch Bartlett Memorial Collection, 1926.224, photograph © 1991, The Art Institute of Chicago. All Rights Reserved.

The Postimpressionists
Seurat and Cézanne

While van Gogh and Gauguin applied color with the abandon of "the civilized savage," the French painter Georges Seurat (d. 1891) treated color as analytically as a modern laboratory technician. Seurat was trained academically, and like the academicians Poussin and David, Seurat brought balance and order to his style. The forms in his compositions, for instance, seem plotted along an invisible graph of vertical and horizontal lines that run parallel to the picture plane. A similar rage for order may have inspired Seurat's novel use of tiny, uniformly sized dots of color, which he applied side by side to build up dense clusters that give the impression of solid form. Since the French word for "dots" is *"points,"* this style is known as *pointillism.* Seurat arrived at the technique of dividing color into component parts after studying the writings of Chevreul and other pioneers in color theory. Leaving nothing to chance (Gauguin called him "the little green chemist"), Seurat analyzed color into its component tints. He applied each tint so that its juxtaposition with the next would produce the desired degree of vibration to the eye of the beholder.

Although Seurat shared the impressionists' fascination with light and color, he preferred tidy formulas to sensuous abandon. He shunned spontaneity and, though he made his sketches out-of-doors, he executed his paintings inside his studio, usually at night and under artificial light.

Seurat's monumental *Sunday Afternoon on the Island of the Grand Jatte* (1886) shows a holiday crowd of Parisians relaxing in a sunlit park (figure 31.22). Although typically impressionistic in its subject matter—French society at leisure—the painting harbors little of the impressionist's love for intimacy and fleeting sensation. Seurat isolates one figure from the next as if each were unaware of the other's existence. One critic railed, "Strip his figures of the colored fleas that cover them; underneath you will find nothing, no thought, no soul." Seurat's universe, with its atomized particles of color and its self-contained figures may seem devoid of human feeling, but, at the same time, its exquisite regularity provides a comforting alternative to the chaos of experience. Indeed, the lasting appeal of *La Grande Jatte* lies in its effectiveness as a symbolic retreat from the tumult of urban life and the accidents of nature.

FIGURE 31.23 *Basket of Apples,* Paul Cézanne, ca. 1895. Oil on canvas, 25 3/4 in. × 32 in. Helen Birch Bartlett Memorial Collection, 1926.252, photograph © 1991, The Art Institute of Chicago. All Rights Reserved.

More so than Seurat, the paintings of Paul Cézanne (d. 1906) served as a bridge between the art of the nineteenth century and that of the twentieth. Cézanne painted such traditional subjects as landscapes, portraits, and still lifes; but, anticipating the art of the next generation, he was more concerned with the formal aspects of the painting than with its contents. For this reason, Cézanne has been called the father of modern art.

Cézanne began his career as an impressionist, but his desire to invest his canvases with a strong sense of three-dimensional solidity and compositional structure (both of which were often ignored by the impressionists) led him to invent a method of building up form by means of small, flat planes of color. Much like Seurat's colored dots, Cézanne's planes provided the substance for his forms and the structure for his compositions. Cézanne's interest in an overall picto-rial unity inspired him to modify traditional methods of reproducing the appearance of physical objects in space: he might, for instance, tilt and flatten surfaces; reduce (or abstract) familiar objects to such basic geometric shapes as cylinders, cones, and spheres; or show each object in the composition from a different point of view. As a result, Cézanne's still lifes are not so much tempting likenesses of apples, peaches, or pears as they are architectural arrangements of colored forms (figure 31.23). A Cézanne still life is a harmonious composition whose measured rhythms and shapes are as intellectually conceived as those of any academic painting. Such a still life fulfilled Cézanne's professed desire to ''redo nature after Poussin,'' that is, to replace the intuitive and sensuous art of the impressionists with paintings that were sturdy, reasoned, and formally composed.

FIGURE 31.24 *Mont Sainte-Victoire,* Paul Cézanne, 1902–04. Oil on canvas, 27 1/2 in. × 35 1/4 in. Philadelphia Museum of Art, George W. Elkins Collection. Acces. E'36–1-1.

Cézanne was discomforted by the hustle and bustle of turn-of-the-century Paris. He chose to live in his native area of Southern France, where he tirelessly painted the local landscape. One of his favorite subjects was the rugged, stony peak of Mont Sainte-Victoire near his hometown of Aix-en-Provence. Among Cézanne's last versions of the subject is a landscape in which trees and houses have become an abstract network of colored facets of paint (figure 31.24). By applying colors of the same intensity to different parts of the canvas—note the bright green and rich violet brushstrokes in both sky and landscape—Cézanne challenged traditional distinctions between foreground and background. Cézanne's methods, which transformed an ordinary mountain into an icon of stability, led the way to modern abstraction.

Summary

Art for art's sake was neither a movement nor a style but rather a prevailing spirit in European and especially French culture of the last quarter of the nineteenth century. In all of the arts, there was a new attention to sensory experience rather than to moral and didactic purpose. At the same time, advances in optics, electricity, and other areas of science and technology brought attention to matters of motion and light. Paralleling new theories of sensation and perception, the philosopher Henri Bergson stressed the role of intuition in grasping the true nature of durational reality. The symbolist poets devised a language that evoked feeling rather than described experience. In Mallarmé's *"L'Apres-midi d'un faune,"* images unfold as sensuous, discontinuous fragments. Similar effects occur in the music of Debussy, where delicately shaded harmonies gently drift without resolution.

The French impressionists, led by Monet, were equally representative of the late nineteenth-century interest in sensation and sensory experience. These artists tried to record an instantaneous vision of their world, sacrificing the details of perceived objects in order to capture the effects of light and atmosphere. Renoir, Degas, Cassatt, and Toulouse-Lautrec produced informal and painterly canvases that offer a glimpse into the pleasures of nineteenth-century European life. Stop-action photographs and the flat, linear designs of Japanese prints influenced the style of the impressionists. Japanese woodcuts also anticipated the decorative style known as art nouveau, which dominated architecture, poster design, and Western arts and crafts in the last decades of the century. In sculpture, the works of Degas and Rodin reflect a common concern for figural gesture and movement. Rodin's efforts to translate inner feelings into expressive forms paralleled Isadora Duncan's innovations in modern dance.

The postimpressionists van Gogh, Gauguin, Seurat, and Cézanne moved away from the impressionist infatuation with fleeting effects. Van Gogh and Gauguin used color not as an atmospheric envelope but as a tool for personal and visionary expression. Seurat and Cézanne reacted against the formlessness of impressionism by creating styles that featured architectural stability and solid, simplified forms. On the threshold of the twentieth century, artists renounced their former roles as idealizers and imitators of nature to assume the liberating challenge of making art for art's sake.

SUGGESTIONS FOR READING

Gogh, van, Vincent. *Van Gogh's Diary": The Artist's Life in His Own Words and Art.* New York: Morrow, 1971.

Goldwater, Robert. *Symbolism.* London: Allen Lane, 1979.

Kroegger, M. E. *Literary Impressionism.* New Haven, Conn.: Yale University Press, 1973.

Masur, Gerhard. *Prophets of Yesterday: Studies in European Culture, 1890–1914.* New York: Macmillan, 1961.

Pevsner, Nikolaus. *Pioneers of Modern Design: From William Morris to Walter Gropius.* New York: Museum of Modern Art, 1949.

Rewald, John. *Cézanne: A Biography.* New York: Abrams, 1986.

————. *The History of Impressionism.* New York: New York Graphic Society, 1980.

Schmutzler, Robert. *Art Nouveau.* New York: Abrams, 1962.

Silverman, Deborah. *Art Nouveau in Fin-de-Siècle France: Politics, Psychology, and Style.* Berkeley: University of California Press, 1989.

MUSIC LISTENING SELECTION

Cassette II Selection 15. Debussy, "Prélude à l'après-midi d'un faune" (1894).

SELECTED GENERAL BIBLIOGRAPHY

Anderson, Bonnie S., and Judith P. Zinsser. *A History of Their Own: Women in Europe from Prehistory to the Present.* Vol. 2. New York: Harper, 1988.

Arnason, H. H. *History of Modern Art: Painting, Sculpture, Architecture, Photography.* 3d ed. New York: Prentice-Hall, 1986.

Artz, F. B. *From the Renaissance to Romanticism: Trends in Style in Art, Literature, and Music, 1300–1830.* Chicago: University of Chicago Press, 1962.

Austin, William. *Music in the Twentieth Century from Debussy through Stravinsky.* New York: Norton, 1966.

Barzun, Jacques. *Darwin, Marx, Wagner: Critique of a Heritage.* Garden City, N.Y.: Doubleday, 1958.

Bridenthal, Renate, and Claudia Koonz, eds. *Becoming Visible: Women in European History.* Boston: Houghton Mifflin, 1977.

Bronowski, Jacob, and Bruce Mazlish. *The Western Intellectual Tradition: From Leonardo to Hegel.* New York: Harper, 1960.

Brown, Calvin S. *Music and Literature: A Comparison of the Arts.* Athens, Ga.: University of Georgia Press, 1948.

Bugner, Ladislas, ed. *The Image of the Black in Western Art.* Vol. 3: *From Sixteenth-Century Europe to Nineteenth-Century America.* Cambridge, Mass.: Harvard University Press, 1986.

Bullock, Alan, and Stephen Trombley. *The Harper Dictionary of Modern Thought.* New York: Harper, 1988.

————, and R. B. Woodbridge, eds. *Modern Culture: A Biographical Companion.* New York: Harper, 1984.

Canaday, John. *Mainstreams of Modern Art.* 2d ed. New York: Holt, Rinehart and Winston, 1981.

Chadwick, Whitney. *Women, Art and Society.* New York: Norton, 1991.

Chang, H. C. *Chinese Literature: Popular Fiction and Drama.* New York: Columbia University Press, 1973.

Clark, Kenneth. *Civilisation: A Personal View.* New York: Harper, 1970.

Clarke, Mary, and Clement Crisp. *The History of Dance.* New York: Crown, 1981.

Copland, Aaron. *What to Listen for in Music.* rev. ed. New York: New American Library, 1957.

Craven, Roy C. *Indian Art.* London: Thames and Hudson, 1976.

Eitner, Lorenz, ed. *Neoclassicism and Romanticism, 1750–1850: An Anthology of Sources and Documents.* New York: Harper, 1989.

Fitzgerald, C. P. *The Horizon History of China.* New York: American Heritage, 1969.

Fleming, William. *Concerts of the Arts: Their Interplay and Modes of Relationship*. Gainesville, Fla.: University of West Florida Press, 1990.

———. *Musical Arts and Styles*. Gainesville, Fla.: University of West Florida Press, 1990.

Harman, Carter. *A Popular History of Music*. rev. ed. New York: Dell, 1973.

Johnson, Paul. *The Birth of the Modern: World Society 1815–1830*. New York: Harper, 1991.

Kaufmann, Walter. *Discovering the Mind*. 3 vols. New York: McGraw-Hill, 1980.

Kostoff, Spiro. *A History of Architecture: Settings and Rituals*. New York: Oxford University Press, 1985.

Lee, Sherman E. *A History of Far Eastern Art*. New York: Abrams, 1964.

Nelson, Lynn H., and Patrick Peebles, eds. *Classics of Eastern Thought*. San Diego: Harcourt, 1991.

Newhall, Beaumont. *The History of Photography: From 1839 to the Present*. rev. ed. New York: Museum of Modern Art, 1982.

Orrey, Leslie. *Opera: A Concise History*. London: Thames and Hudson, 1968.

Pevsner, Nikolaus. *An Outline of European Architecture*. 6th ed. Baltimore, Md.: Penguin, 1960.

Raynor, Henry. *A Social History of Music: From the Middle Ages to Beethoven*. New York: Schocken Books, 1972.

Russell, Bertrand. *A History of Western Philosophy*. 2d ed. New York: Simon and Schuster, 1984.

Sadie, Stanley, ed. *The New Grove Dictionary of Music and Musicians*. New York: Macmillan, 1980.

Sorrell, Walter. *The Dance Through the Ages*. New York: Grosset and Dunlap, 1967.

Spence, Jonathan D. *The Search for Modern China*. New York: Norton, 1990.

Sterling, Charles. *Still Life Painting from Antiquity to the Twentieth Century*. 2d rev. ed. New York: Harper, 1981.

Sypher, Wylie. *Rococo to Cubism in Art and Literature*. New York: Random House, 1960.

Weiss, Piero, and Richard Taruskin. *Music in the Western World: A History in Documents*. New York: Schirmer Books, 1984.

Wiener, Philip P., ed. *Dictionary of the History of Ideas*. New York: Scribners, 1973.

Books in Series

Great Ages of Man. A History of the World's Cultures. New York: Time, Inc., 1965–69.

Library of Art Series. New York: Time-Life Books, Inc., 1967.

Time-Frame. 25 vols. (projected). New York: Time-Life Books, 1990–.

CREDITS

Chapter 27

Reading 95 (pp. 7–8): Excerpt from "Lines Composed a Few Miles Above Tintern Abbey" by Wordsworth, in *The College Survey of English Literature,* Shorter Edition, Revised by Alexander Witherspoon, reprinted by permission of Harcourt Brace Jovanovich, Inc.

Reading 96 (p. 9): Excerpt from "Ode to the West Wind" by Shelley, in *The College Survey of English Literature,* Shorter Edition, Revised by Alexander Witherspoon, reprinted by permission of Harcourt Brace Jovanovich, Inc.

Reading 97 (p. 11): Excerpt from "Ode on a Grecian Urn" by Keats, in *The College Survey of English Literature,* Shorter Edition, Revised by Alexander Witherspoon, reprinted by permission of Harcourt Brace Jovanovich, Inc.

Reading 98 (p. 12): From Henry David Thoreau, *Walden,* Airmont Classics edition. Copyright © Thomas Bouregy & Company, Inc., New York, New York. Reprinted by permission.

Reading 99 (pp. 13–14): From Walt Whitman, *Leaves of Grass,* 1900. Source: David McKay, Philadelphia.

Chapter 28

Map 28.1 (p. 20): From *Civilization: Past & Present,* Volume 2, 8/e by T. Walter Wallbank, et al. Copyright © 1981, 1976 by Scott, Foresman and Company. Reprinted by permission of HarperCollins Publishers.

Reading 100 (p. 22): Excerpted from *The Corsican: A Diary of Napoleon's Life in His Own Words,* 1910. Boston: Houghton Mifflin Company.

Reading 102 (pp. 25–32): From *Goethe's Faust,* Parts I and II, translated by Louis MacNeice. Copyright 1951, 1943 by Frederick Louis MacNeice; renewed 1979 by Hedli MacNeice. Reprinted by permission of Oxford University Press, Inc., New York and David Higham Associates, Ltd., London.

Reading 103 (p. 32): Reprinted from *Heinrich Heine: Lyric Poems and Ballads* by Heinrich Heine, translated by Ernst Feise, by permission of the University of Pittsburgh Press. © 1961 by University of Pittsburgh Press.

Chapter 30

Map 30.1 (p. 65): Figure from *The Mainstream of Civilization, Since 1660,* Part Two, Second Edition by Joseph Strayer, copyright © 1974 by Harcourt Brace Jovanovich, Inc., reprinted by permission of the publisher.

Reading 104 (pp. 69–71): From Frederick Engel and Karl Marx, *The Communist Manifesto,* translated by Samuel Moore, revised and edited by Frederick Engel for the 1888 English edition.

Reading 105 (pp. 71–72): From John Stuart Mill, *The Subjection of Women.* (Buffalo, N.Y.: Prometheus Books). Reprinted by permission of the publisher.

Reading 106 (p. 73): Charles Dickens, *The Old Curiosity Shop.*

Reading 107 (p. 74–75): From *Madame Bovary* by G. Flaubert, trans. by F. Steegmuller. Translation Copyright © 1957 by Francis Steegmuller. Reprinted by permission of Random House, Inc.

Reading 108 (pp. 76–77): From *Six Plays by Henrik Ibsen* by Henrik Ibsen, trans. by Eva Le Gallienne. Copyright © 1957 by Eva Le Gallienne. Reprinted by permission of Random House, Inc.

Figure 30.9 (p. 81): From Richard Phipps and Richard Wink, *Invitation to the Gallery.* Copyright © 1987 Wm. C. Brown Publishers, Dubuque, Iowa. All Rights Reserved. Reprinted by permission.

Chapter 31

Reading 109 (pp. 92–93): "The Afternoon of a Faun" in *The Poetry of Mallarmé.* Copyright © 1952 HarperCollins Publishers, Inc., New York. Copyright © 1952 The Estate of Aldous Huxley, Mrs. Laura Huxley, and Random Century Group, London.

Line Art

Alice Thiede
Map 28.1 (p. 20)
Map 30.1 (p. 65)

INDEX

〜〜〜

Titles of works are set in *italics* with the artist/author's name in parentheses. Page numbers of illustrations are in **boldface** type.

A

Adventures of Huckleberry Finn (Twain), 72
Africa, 65, 67
Afternoon of a Faun. See "Après-midi"
Age of Bronze (Rodin), 104, **105**
Agnew Clinic (Eakins), 87, **87**
Aida (Verdi), 60
Anarchism, 68
Anthony, Susan B., 71
"Après-midi d'un faune," (Mallarmé), 92–93 (text), 113
Arabs Skirmishing in the Mountains (Delacroix), **46**, 47
Arch of Triumph (Chalgrin), 48
Architecture
    American, 64
    art nouveau, 103
    neomedieval, 50, 51, 61
    and technology, 51–52, 64
Aristotle, 15
Art
    Chinese, 35
    impressionist, 93–102, 103–6
    Japanese, 100–101
    postimpressionist, 107–12
    realist, 77–89
    romantic, 35–51

Art nouveau, 103
Artist's Letter Rack, The (Harnett), 86, **86**
At the Moulin-Rouge (Toulouse-Lautrec), 102, **102**

B

Ballet. *See* Dance
Barry, Charles, 50
Bartholdi, Frederic-Auguste, 48
Basket of Apples (Cézanne), **111**
Bath, The (Cassatt), 101, **101**
Beethoven, Ludwig van, 4, 21, 53–55, 56, 61; Music Listening Selection II–11
Bentham, Jeremy, 68
Bergson, Henri, 91, 92, 113
Berlioz, Hector, 4, 55–56, 61; Music Listening Selection II–13
Bierstadt, Albert, 42, 61
Bizet, Georges, 32
Bohème, La (Puccini), 89, 90
Boucher, François, 83
Brady, Mathew B., 78, 87
Brahms, Johannes, 55
Brontë, Emily, 33
Brothers Karamazov, The (Dostoevsky), 74
Brueghel, Pieter, 35
Buddhism, 12
Burial at Ornans, The (Courbet), 81, **81**
Byron, George Gordon, Lord, 4, 22–23, 34, 46, 53, 59

C

Capitalism, 66, 68, 69
Caravaggio (Michelangelo Merici), 46
Carlyle, Thomas, 19
Carpeaux, Jean Baptiste, 58
Cassatt, Mary, 97, 101, 102, 113
Catlin, George, 42
Cézanne, Paul, 4, 97, 110, 111–12, 113
Champs Elysées, 48
Charles IV, King of Spain, 44
Chevreul, Michel, 94, 110
Childe Harold's Pilgrimage (Byron), 22, 55
China
    painting of, 35
    poetry of, 8
    and the West, 65, 67
Chopin, Frederic, 4, 33, 56, 57, 61; Music Listening Selection II–14
Civil War. *See* War
Clemens, Samuel Langhorne. *See* Twain, Mark
Code Napoleon, 20
Cole, Thomas, 41, 61
Colonialism, 63, 65, 67
Communism, 69–71, 90
Communist Manifesto (Marx and Engels), 68, 68–69, 69–71 (text), 90
Constable, John, 4, 36, 37, 39, 61, 95
Cooper, James Fenimore, 11
Copernicus, Nicolas, 5
Corot, Jean-Baptiste-Camille, 40, 57, 61
Country School, The (Homer), 87, **88**
Courbet, Gustave, 4, 79, 80, 81, 85, 90